WHOLE RELATIONSHIPS

How Imperfect People Create Unbroken Love

How Imperfect People Create Unbroken Love

by

Annette R. Purkiss

Atlanta, GA

Whole Relationships: How Imperfect People Create Unbroken Love

For more info, contact the publisher at:
Allwrite Publishing
1445 Woodmont Lane NW #495
Atlanta, GA 30318
info@allwritepublishing.com

ISBN: 978-1-941716-36-6 (hardback)
ISBN: 978-1-941716-37-3 (paperback)
ISBN: 978-1-941716-38-0 (ebook)

Printed in the United States of America

Library of Congress Cataloging-in-Publication Data

Names: Johnson, Annette R. author
Title: Whole relationships : how imperfect people create unbroken love / by Annette R. Purkiss.
Description: Atlanta, GA : Allwrite Publishing, [2025] | Includes bibliographical references. | Summary: “In Whole Relationships, Annette R. Purkiss offers a compassionate, faith-centered roadmap for transforming patterns of brokenness into practices of wholeness. Drawing from psychology, scripture, and lived experience, she shows that healthy relationships begin not with finding the right person, but with becoming whole in ourselves and then with others. In it, you learn that love isn’t meant to be perfect; it’s meant to be whole. Through honest stories, reflective prompts, and spiritual insight, Purkiss helps readers set boundaries without guilt, practice courageous vulnerability, and stop chasing validation. The result is love grounded in purpose, peace, and mutual respect, a love made whole”-- Provided by publisher.
Identifiers: LCCN 2025050547 (print) | LCCN 2025050548 (ebook) | ISBN 9781941716366 hardback | ISBN 9781941716373 paperback | ISBN 9781941716380 epub
Subjects: LCSH: Interpersonal relations--Religious aspects--Christianity
Classification: LCC BV4597.52 .J64 2025 (print) | LCC BV4597.52 (ebook)
LC record available at https://lccn.loc.gov/2025050547
LC ebook record available at https://lccn.loc.gov/2025050548

DEDICATION

To everything and everyone in my past that shaped my wholeness

CONTENTS

PART III

THE SOUL ESSENTIALS

PART IV

THE T.O.R.C.H. OF LOVE

PART V

THE PRACTICE OF WHOLE LOVE

APPENDICES

PREFACE

I want to be clear about something from the beginning: none of the relationships that shaped this work ended because love was absent. There was love. There was commitment. In some cases, there was even a willingness to try again. What was missing was wholeness, not affection, attraction or effort. Over time, I learned that the feeling of love, by itself, cannot repair broken patterns, resolve unspoken fears, or sustain intimacy without awareness and accountability. Money, success, and even spiritual devotion cannot substitute for the inner work required to show up whole. I wrote this book because I wish someone had taught me that love is not the foundation of a healthy relationship – wholeness is.

The objective of this book is for readers to discover and experience something I had never fully known: a healthy, whole relationship with myself and others. That truth became painfully clear during a relationship in which I had to keep shrinking to make it work.

From childhood, I learned that other people's needs mattered more than mine. I became skilled at accommodating, at keeping the peace, and at minimizing myself except when something crossed an obvious line. I knew how to express anger in the face of blatant disrespect, but I did not yet know how to assert my deeper soul needs.

In that relationship, I carried far more of the emotional weight than I realized at the time. I initiated communication, made plans, and sustained the connection with very little reciprocation. When I tried to express my needs — such as wanting to see each other consistently — they were dismissed or redefined in ways that left me questioning my own reality. In order to preserve the connection, I learned to quiet myself.

I allowed this dynamic to continue for nearly two years because I was not being honest with myself. I had slowly abandoned my own needs in exchange for intermittent attention. With hindsight, I recognized this as a familiar pattern in my life, one rooted in brokenness.

When I finally chose to step back and disengage, the response was not curiosity or reassurance, but distance and dismissal. The loss was painful, but it was also clarifying. I knew then that what I needed was not reconciliation, but healing and the courage to become whole.

As I began that healing, I gained clarity about the relational dynamics at play. Understanding emotional unavailability helped me release resentment and extend forgiveness, but my focus remained where it belonged: on myself, and on why I had repeatedly outsourced my sense of wholeness to others.

Many people aren't bad at love. They're operating from unexamined patterns that were never designed to sustain intimacy. So, this book is for those who, like me, have allowed childhood wounds or adult betrayals to fracture their sense of self. It is for those who have discovered that constantly accommodating, people-pleasing, blaming others, or erupting in frustration no longer leads to peace or connection. It is also for those who have gone into overprotection mode, becoming hypervigilant, guarded, or emotionally distant in order to feel safe. For those who struggle with poor communication, unrealistic expectations, unresolved trauma, and so forth, this wholeness journey can provide tools to develop healthy, whole patterns.

Whole Relationships is an invitation to return to who you are when you stop performing for acceptance or running for safety and start living from truth. This work is about meeting yourself honestly, because showing up as you — whole, aware, and grounded — is the surest way to build healthy, sustaining relationships and elevate every area of your life.

What began as a painful ending became the beginning of my awakening. I learned that love cannot be whole if it requires you to abandon or erase yourself. The journey that follows — through every framework, reflection, and story in this book — is about reclaiming what you may have given away in pieces and learning to live and love from the inside out.

This book is meant to be read slowly and lived gently. Some chapters are designed to awaken awareness; others invite practice. You do not need to understand everything at once, and you do not need to change everything immediately.

For this reason, a companion workbook exists, not to add work, but to reduce pressure. When reflection or practice will serve you more than continued reading, I will invite you to pause and use it. These pauses are not detours; they are part of the whole relationships journey.

Enjoy!

Annette

NOTE ON HOW TO USE THIS BOOK

This book is meant to be read slowly and lived gently. Some chapters are designed to awaken awareness; others invite practice. You do not need to understand everything at once, and you do not need to change everything immediately.

For this reason, a companion workbook exists, not to add work, but to reduce pressure. When reflection or practice will serve you more than continued reading, I will invite you to pause and use it. These pauses are not detours; they are part of the journey.

Throughout the book, you will see a small set of visual guides placed at intentional moments. These are not instructions to rush or perform something, but invitations to listen, reflect, or slow down when needed. Thus, you may encounter these four icons to help direct you to necessary resources and resets:

Practice Guide — an invitation to pause and engage the companion workbook	
Wholeness Pause — a moment to stop reading and let something settle	
Reflection Moment — a question or invitation for journaling or quiet thought	
Discernment Marker — a gentle signal to proceed slowly and thoughtfully	

As a signal for key questions, you may see this icon used at times: 

Paying attention to these guides will help you move through this journey with greater clarity, care, and compassion for yourself and for others.

COMPLETE ME, THE INTRODUCTION

"You complete me" is often quoted by those expressing their love and commitment to another. Yet, if that statement is true, you're already asking for trouble in your relationship. Love was never meant to complete us. It was meant to *complement* who we already are. Thus, our goal is to ensure that two imperfect, whole people come together to form a *whole relationship*.

We focus on two key principles in developing what we call a *whole relationship*:

- **Connection** — with self and others
- **Commitment** — to self and others

An unbroken, or *whole*, relationship is not perfect. It involves two imperfect people who are self-aware, surrendered, and willing to serve one another's soul needs. It captures the truth that a whole relationship isn't about perfection; it's about intention, humility, and mutual service.

To expand slightly:

- **Imperfect, perhaps broken people** — Everyone comes into relationships with wounds, flaws, and history. Wholeness doesn't mean being without pain; it means being honest about it.
- **Self-aware** — Self-awareness is the foundation of emotional maturity. It allows each person to recognize their triggers, take responsibility for their emotions, and grow.
- **Surrendered** — This reflects the condition of one's heart: willing to rely fully on God and look to each other for understanding.
- **Servanthood** — This involves mutual respect, consideration, and appreciation so that both partners feel seen, supported, and fulfilled.

Servanthood in whole love is not submission without boundaries or self-erasure. It is mutual willingness expressed through responsibility for one another's core needs. Ultimately, it is the disciplined choice to care for another without neglecting oneself.

A relationship is "healthy" when it functions well. It is "whole" when the people within it live in alignment. The aim of this book is to cultivate healthy, whole relationships.

Whole Relationships are formed, not found. Through awareness, surrender, and service, we transform brokenness into bonding and pain into purpose. In this book, I introduce three models that capture the essence of whole relationships:

- **Self-Aware** — *ARC of Self*
- **Surrendered** — *TORCH of Love*
- **Servanthood** — *Soul Needs*

The order of the book's main themes reflects a natural progression of whole growth:

1. **ARC of Self** → explores the inner work required for wholeness
2. **Soul Needs** → reveals the deeper motivations and needs that shape how we relate to ourselves and others
3. **TORCH of Love** → teaches how whole people express love through trust, openness, respect, communication, and humility

Together these frameworks form the foundation of **whole love**, a love that is aligned, authentic, spiritually grounded, and emotionally mature. These three postures take practical shape in the associated models you'll explore in the book. Before we begin, it helps to understand the two outcomes this journey is designed to produce.

First, this book invites you to become a whole person. Whole love begins as an individual identity before it becomes a relational practice. Through the ARC of Self and the discovery of Soul Needs, you will learn to live with greater self-awareness, self-respect, self-confidence, emotional maturity, and spiritual grounding. The goal is not simply to improve your relationships, but to become the kind of person who can thrive in a healthy, whole relationship. In other words, the first outcome is personal: **This is who I become before I become one with someone else.**

Second, this book teaches how whole love is practiced in relationship. Once a person learns to live aligned within themselves, they can begin expressing that wholeness through connection, communication, humility, repair, and commitment. This is where the TORCH of Love comes to life, guiding how two people build trust, navigate conflict, and sustain intimacy over time.

These two outcomes form the foundation of whole relationships: becoming whole within and practicing whole love with others.

This book doesn't teach you *how to attract people*; it teaches you *how attraction affects* your ability to experience whole relationships. It helps readers transform patterns of brokenness into practices of wholeness. The book demonstrates how the individual journey of healing (self-work) evolves into mutual wholeness (soul service). Essentially, it's where *personal healing* culminates in *shared transformation.* The emotional and spiritual path of the *Whole Relationships* journey is from brokenness to wholeness, from self to service, from love as longing to love as becoming.

It is for singles, couples, and those healing from heartbreak, guiding you toward love that is mature, mindful, and mutual. Each section blends spiritual insight, emotional intelligence, and practical exercises grounded in the **ARC of Self**, **TORCH of Love**, and **Soul Needs Model**. Together, these create the foundation for **whole relationships**, where imperfect people learn to love with wholeness, grace, and divine intention.

The journey to whole love begins with the heart, expands through the mind, and matures in the soul. Part I invites you to start the journey from brokenness to wholeness, which begins in the heart that's willing to tell the truth. Let's start there.

Before continuing, however, take a moment to ground yourself. Wholeness begins with awareness, not urgency. If you have the *Whole Relationships Workbook*, I encourage you to complete the opening pages now. They are designed to help you locate where you are before we explore where you're going. There is no right starting point, only an honest one.

PART I

THE HEART OF WHOLENESS

From Broken to Whole

1

LOVE ISN'T PERFECT, BUT IT CAN BE WHOLE

We live in a culture obsessed with perfection, including perfect bodies, perfect careers, and perfect relationships. The myth of perfect love tells us that when we meet the "right" person, everything will simply fall into place. However, real love doesn't "fall" anywhere; it's built, shaped over time through intention and repair.

Many people enter relationships hoping love will fix what feels incomplete or imperfect within them. Yet wholeness does not begin between two people; it begins within a person. Wholeness must begin *within* before it can exist *between*. Only when a person learns to live aligned with truth can they be in a healthy and whole relationship.

This reflects a core truth of *Whole Relationships*: love is about intention, not perfection. It is sustained through honesty, humility, and the willingness to repair. Love becomes whole not through flawless performance, but through faithful practice. As explored in *What's Your Motivation?* (Johnson, 2026), our love is only as whole as the motives behind it. Intentional love doesn't just seek connection; it seeks clarity of purpose, ensuring that affection isn't driven by fear, validation, or self-interest, but by conscious alignment with truth and care.

When we shift from perfection to intention, we realize that love isn't about fixing others or finding someone who completes us. It begins with becoming whole ourselves. Yet wholeness is often confused with healing, and though the two are related, they are not the same.

What It Means to Be "Whole" vs. "Healed"

Healing and wholeness are related, but they are not the equivalent. Healing often focuses on recovery, closing wounds and reducing pain. Sometimes it even centers on other people's shortcomings or faults, measuring our progress by how much we've distanced ourselves from those who hurt us.

Wholeness goes further, though. It's about **integration.** It allows every part of who you are – your strengths, scars, lessons, and longing – to coexist in harmony. Instead of centering on what someone else did or failed to do, wholeness invites responsibility over resentment and alignment over avoidance.

Healing asks, *"What hurt me, and how do I make it stop?"*

Wholeness asks, *"What shaped me, and how do I live aligned with truth now?"*

Healing is about recovery, but wholeness is about revelation, living aligned with who you truly are or who you're becoming. "Alignment" simply means that your beliefs, values, and behaviors are working together instead of fighting each other, so that who you are on the inside matches how you live on the outside. It looks like saying yes when you mean yes, no when you mean no, and acting in ways that reflect what you truly believe. Healing focuses on relief while wholeness focuses on alignment. Simply put: Healing restores stability. Wholeness restores identity.

In Scripture, Christ didn't just heal people physically; He restored them relationally and spiritually, bringing them back into alignment with truth. In the same way, wholeness means living from the inside out, where what you do reflects who you are. Integrated truth produces integrity of life. Scripture reminds us that truth is not merely information; it is liberation: "You will know the truth, and the truth will set you free" (John 8:32). Wholeness is not achieved by avoiding reality, but by living honestly within it.

We will return to this distinction throughout the book, particularly as we define wholeness more fully and explore what it looks like in daily life.

If you notice grief, resistance, or relief as you read this distinction, pause. Consider what you may have been trying to "heal away" rather than integrate, and explore it in your journal.

Wholeness as a Spiritual and Psychological Process

Wholeness integrates the spiritual, the psychological, and the relational. It involves learning to:

- See yourself truthfully (self-awareness)
- Surrender ego and fear (trust and humility)
- Serve with love and integrity (mutuality)

Psychologically, this aligns with secure attachment, where emotional safety and honesty coexist. Spiritually, it reflects the call to "love your neighbor as yourself" (Matt. 22:39; Mark 12:31). You can't offer what you haven't first cultivated within. In both psychology and Scripture, healthy relationships grow from internal alignment rather than external perfection.

One of the world's leading relationship researchers, Dr. John Gottman, found that lasting couples don't avoid conflict; they manage it constructively. What distinguishes healthy relationships from unhealthy ones isn't the absence of problems, but the presence of repair. His research shows that successful couples respond to each other's emotional "bids" for connection with care and attention rather than criticism or defensiveness (Gottman & Silver, 2015).

Dr. Gottman emphasizes this further through his "Sound Relationship House Theory," which teaches that healthy love is built on layers of trust, commitment, shared meaning, and emotional attunement (Gottman 1994). These principles mirror spiritual growth: awareness leads to humility, humility leads to service, and service sustains connection.

When relationship science and spiritual truth are viewed together, wholeness appears less mystical and more practical. It is not a personality trait or a spiritual achievement. It is a daily practice of emotional stewardship guided by divine alignment. These concepts will be explored in greater depth as we move through the ARC of Self and the practice of whole love.

The Three Conditions of a Whole Relationship

For love to be whole rather than fragile, three internal conditions must be cultivated:

Self-Awareness is the foundation of connection. It is the courage to look inward and name your truth without shame. Awareness interrupts cycles of projection and blame, allowing you to take responsibility for your inner life.

Surrender is the posture that makes growth possible. It is not weakness, but wisdom. Surrender releases control, entitlement, and fear. Spiritually, it is trusting God's process. Relationally, it is trusting that honesty will lead to clarity, even when it is uncomfortable.

Servanthood is love expressed in action. It honors both people in the relationship. Servanthood is not submission or self-erasure; it is mutuality, empathy, and purpose.

Wholeness requires all three. Awareness keeps us *honest*, surrender keeps us *humble*, and servanthood keeps us *connected.* Together, they make love not perfect, but whole. Thus, a Whole Relationship is not built on perfection but on awareness, surrender, and service. It joins two imperfect souls who are self-aware enough to grow, surrendered enough to trust, and servant-hearted enough to love. These conditions will be revisited and practiced throughout this book.

Wholeness in Practice: The Life of David

King David is one of Scripture's clearest examples of wholeness, not because he lived perfectly, but because he lived *honestly, humbly,* and *aligned with God's heart.* He is often remembered for his moral lapse with Bathsheba and his moments of anger and impulsiveness. Yet Scripture still describes him as "a man after God's own heart" (1 Samuel 13:14). That description has little to do with perfection and everything to do with the posture of his soul. David was profoundly *self-aware*; the moment he recognized his wrong, he brought it before God without excuse or pretense. He lived a *surrendered* life, constantly seeking God's direction and protection. He *served* both God and the people he led by honoring God's statutes and returning, again and again, to the foundation of his faith.

Some may judge David through the lens of his mistakes and label him broken. However, God saw him as whole because his heart remained open, honest, and aligned. Wholeness isn't the absence of missteps; it's the presence of sincerity, accountability, and a willingness to be guided. David's life shows us that even when we stumble, a self-aware, surrendered, servant heart keeps us connected to the God who restores.

David's life reminds us that wholeness does not come from self-sufficiency or moral flawlessness, but from remaining open to love, correction, and restoration. His strength was not rooted in self-sufficiency or self-trust. It came from relationship. This challenges one of the most common assumptions in modern conversations about healing and love: the belief that love begins within us, fully formed and independent of relationship.

The Myth of Self-Love

"Love yourself first" is what we often hear from those offering advice on relationships. Love is not self-generated, though. When this fact is overlooked, love is treated as something that exists apart from relationship rather than within it.

> ***"Love is not the foundation of a healthy relationship, wholeness is."***

Suggesting that we are love and don't need others (relationships) to feel or express love is shortsighted. First, God is love, not us. Second, humans have *hope in* love, and when we meet someone we like or are attracted to, that person becomes the object of that hope, or *faith* in love. We can see this more clearly in raising children: if we never show them love through touch, support, and presence, they never truly feel loved or develop faith in love.

Western culture often teaches that the highest form of love is self-love such that we must look inward, affirm ourselves, and become our own source of worth. However, this assumes something that isn't actually true: love can be generated in isolation. In reality, self-love is not something we invent from nothing; it is something we *learn* through being loved first.

If a person has never been genuinely loved – being seen, accepted, cared for, and treated as having inherent worth – they have no reference point for what love actually is. Asking them to "love themselves" is like asking someone to speak a language they've never heard. At best, self-love becomes imitation or performance; at worst, it turns into self-protection, self-obsession, or numbness rather than true care for the self.

Love is relational by nature. We come to understand our value because someone else first treated us as valuable. Over time, those experiences are internalized, allowing us to extend expressions of love (e.g. consideration, compassion, and patience) to ourselves. Without that foundation, self-love is not empowerment; it's an abstraction. True self-love grows out of received love, not apart from it.

For this reason, Whole Relationships focuses not on self-love, but on self-connection and commitment, a framework we'll return to throughout this book. We explain what this means, why it's important and how to implement it.

This isn't about how to *find* love, because it's a gift we both give and receive. So, we don't seek love. Instead, we seek to remove the barriers we have built against love. Love must be allowed, maintained and grown. So, this whole love journey is about acknowledging and removing the barriers from having a healthy, whole connection and commitment to oneself and others. The goal is to **let love flow thoroughly**.

When love is misunderstood as something we must generate and maintain alone, the natural result is not wholeness, but strain. We begin performing wellness, protecting ourselves from disappointment or calling isolation "strength." What we label as self-love often emerges as a response to wounds that were never acknowledged, named, or tended. Before we can remove the barriers to love, we must first understand how they were built. That requires an honest look at brokenness, not as a label of shame, but as a condition shaped by unmet needs, unresolved pain, and learned defenses.

That is where our journey continues.

2

BROKENNESS: HOW WE LOSE OURSELVES IN LOVE

Brokenness rarely announces itself. It forms quietly through experiences that fracture safety, distort self-worth, or teach us to survive by shrinking. Over time, what began as protection becomes pattern.

We do not wake up one day intending to lose ourselves in love. We lose ourselves slowly through unmet needs, misplaced trust, and beliefs formed in moments when we did not yet have the language to understand what was happening. Brokenness is not weakness. It is adaptation.

Ways We Become Broken

Brokenness usually doesn't happen all at once. It's a series of moments that chip away at our sense of worth, safety, or belonging. Sometimes it occurs slowly or sometimes in one shattering blow. It can begin in childhood and continue through the many roles we play as adults.

We become broken when:

In Childhood

- We are told to "be quiet" when we try to express how we feel.
- We learn that love has to be earned, including through grades, obedience or performance.
- We grow up too soon, caring for parents or siblings instead of being cared for.
- A parent leaves through abandonment, incarceration, or death and we never fully understand why.
- We experience abuse, neglect, or the emotional absence of someone who was physically there.

- We're made to feel invisible because we're "different" — too loud, too quiet, too dark, too light, too creative, too sensitive, etc.

In Relationships

- We give everything to someone who gives nothing back.
- We mistake attention for affection, and attachment for love.
- We stay after betrayal, believing our forgiveness will fix what's broken.
- We're manipulated into silence, told that our boundaries make us "selfish."
- We lose ourselves trying to keep the relationship intact.
- We love addicts, caretaking them into our own exhaustion.
- We become an addict to substances, people or validation in order to numb what we can't control.

In Family and Friendship

- We play the "strong one" so long that no one sees our pain.
- We carry generational burdens that were never ours to hold.
- We outgrow people we thought would grow with us.
- We forgive without repair, hoping love alone will make things right.

In Work and Purpose

- We are fired or overlooked after giving our all and start to question our value.
- Our creativity is dismissed, our voice minimized, our ideas taken.
- We compromise integrity for approval or a paycheck.
- We lose passion for something that once defined us.

Through Loss and Change

- Someone we love dies, and the world feels permanently uneven.
- A dream collapses, and we wonder who we are without it.
- We move, divorce, retire, or age, and part of us feels left behind.
- We survive but forget how to live.

Brokenness doesn't always look like pain. Sometimes it looks like numbness. Sometimes it looks like success. We smile, we function, we achieve, but inside, something essential has been silenced. Recognizing the places where we've been broken isn't about shame; it's about reclaiming the pieces of ourselves that still deserve to be whole.

If memories from childhood, family, or past relationships surface as you read these examples, pause here, and continue this reflection in your journal.

How Brokenness Shows Up

When we carry unresolved pain, it begins to express itself in ways that damage our relationships, our decisions and even our self-worth. Brokenness rarely stays hidden; it simply finds other ways to speak. Sometimes it's easily detected, but other times it lies dormant, only to be triggered by a familiar tone, face or feeling that reminds us of an old wound. When we are unaware of these roots, we may confuse symptoms for personality or survival mechanisms for strength. In any case, brokenness left unaddressed always seeks expression through what we do, say, avoid or attract.

Here are ways that brokenness:

1. Risky and Self-Destructive Behavior

- **Sexual incontinence or promiscuity** — seeking connection through physical intimacy to fill emotional voids
- **Substance abuse or binge behaviors** — numbing the ache of emptiness or rejection
- **Reckless decision-making** — acting impulsively to feel powerful or alive when internally disconnected

2. Behavioral and Social Disruption

- **Delinquent behavior** — defying authority or social norms as a way of reclaiming lost control
- **Chronic conflict** — repeatedly engaging in toxic relationships, arguments, or cycles of drama
- **Aggression or verbal abuse** — lashing out as protection from vulnerability or perceived rejection

3. Emotional and Psychological Effects

- **Depression and hopelessness** — feeling that life has no purpose or that healing isn't possible
- **Emotional suppression** — appearing "strong" or "fine" while disconnected from true feelings
- **Anxiety and hypervigilance** — always anticipating hurt or abandonment
- **Low self-worth** — believing we're undeserving of love, respect, or good things

4. Relationship and Commitment Challenges

- **Aversion to marriage or long-term commitment** — fearing emotional dependence or repeating past pain
- **Cynicism about love** — expecting disappointment, betrayal, or failure
- **Codependency** — defining self-worth through someone else's needs or approval
- **Isolation or withdrawal** — avoiding closeness to protect against potential heartbreak

5. Academic and Professional Struggles

- **Behavioral or learning problems in school** — difficulty focusing or trusting authority figures
- **Underachievement** — sabotaging success due to fear of visibility or failure
- **Financial despair** — impulsive spending, dependency, or cycles of debt tied to emotional instability
- **Workplace dysfunction** — difficulty with collaboration, feedback, or consistency due to unresolved wounds

What situation, person, or season of life fractured something in you? For many people, brokenness doesn't arrive all at once. It builds through losses we didn't expect, betrayals we didn't see coming, disappointments we weren't prepared for, or wounds from childhood that quietly follow us into adulthood. It might be the death of someone you loved, a breakup that reshaped your identity, a deception that stole your sense of safety, an abandonment that left you doubting your worth, or even a job-related setback that shook your confidence. The residual effects of these experiences may linger at the surface, demanding our attention. Meanwhile, others sink deep, becoming memories we try to bury but never quite escape. You can usually tell if something is still affecting you when your life continues to orbit around it in some way – when its emotional gravity hasn't loosened its hold. For example, you may find yourself:

- Thinking about it often
- Talking about it often
- Emotionally reacting to it often (crying, anger, withdrawal)
- Blaming it often
- Spending excessive time on it
- Spending excessive money on it

Brokenness is not a permanent condition, but it can become a pattern if ignored or denied. These effects are not our identity, though. They are evidence of where our hearts still need care. Recognizing them isn't about judgment; it's about awareness. Because what we name, we can begin to change. For a quick check-in, take the "**Brokenness Diagnostic Quiz**" (**Appendix A**).

If you recognize yourself in any of these patterns, pause before continuing. In your journal, write without judgment about what these behaviors may have been protecting you from.

Brokenness vs. Wholeness

Brokenness shields you from the truth, allowing you to believe a misconception or lie that you now live with as truth. False beliefs can literally terrorize us, as what we think affects every area of our lives, and most importantly, our actions and reactions.

Brokenness has a way of shaping how we see the world and ourselves. It colors our interpretations, distorts our expectations, and influences the choices we make – often without our awareness. Wholeness doesn't erase our history, but it does reorient our perspective. It shifts us from reacting out of old wounds to responding from a place of clarity and truth. The contrast becomes clear when you look at how each mindset approaches everyday life. Here are some examples:

Broken	**Whole**
Pretend to have all the answers	Acknowledge you don't know the answer
Focus on the rules without regard to their effect	Focus on the effect of the rules
Believe money defines people	Believe money exposes people
Focus on what you don't have	Focus on what you do have
Blame others for most of their shortcomings	Accept responsibility for their choices

Broken people have allowed these lies or false beliefs to overcome them. Thus, they live as they were never meant, separated from their true essence and purpose. They are slaves to some destructive belief or feeling that causes them to act and react in unproductive ways, typically hurting themselves or those around them.

When we are broken, we may "stuff" the holes in our lives with things, activities or people to make us feel unbroken. This "stuffing" occurs both consciously and unconsciously. One of my longtime client's wife of 50 years died, and after her death, her husband went back to work immediately. I asked him why so soon, and he said it was the only way he could "feel normal" and avoid thinking about his wife so much. The death of his wife had caused him emotional brokenness, and instead of properly going through the stages of grief, he chose the stuff the holes in his heart with work.

Wholeness doesn't mean you're perfect. It means you recognize and reject lies that once hindered you or could be hindering you from the truth of who you are. Will those lies keep trying to return and disrupt your life? Yes, but whole people know what and how to fight them.

"Brokenness is not weakness. It's adaptation."

The Masquerade

Sometimes masquerading as wholeness is what we deem as "success," including having a:

- Great Job
- Thriving Career
- Nuclear Family
- Stellar Reputation
- Influential Position

Many times, there are very broken people behind all the fame, money and power. In fact, these individuals may believe that these trappings of success can fill the voids in their lives. How many times have we heard stories of rich people who take their own lives either directly (suicide) or indirectly (destructive lifestyle)?

The person who lives in a small trailer or hut may have more wholeness than someone who lives in a mansion or high-priced condo. Thus, wholeness is determined by your character, not your circumstances, attitude or altitude. Sometimes masquerading as brokenness is what we deem as failure, including:

- Losing a Contest
- Getting Fired or Dumped
- Being Rejected or Overlooked
- Having Few Friends
- Struggling in School

Failure doesn't constitute brokenness, however. The great teacher failure provides opportunities for the wise and only anguish for the foolish. Furthermore, it builds character, and the greatest of these effects would be humility. In achieving a whole healthy relationship, it requires humility.

Discernment: Knowing What's Yours to Carry

Potential shows you what someone *could* be; patterns show you who they *are*. Don't fall in love with someone's potential; fall in love with their patterns. People reveal themselves through consistency, not through promises. Hope may blind you, but patterns will teach you. God often shows us the truth early, but we stay because we fall in love with the idea of who we want them to become instead of the evidence of who they have already chosen to be.

It's better to wait for the right person than to waste time with the wrong one wishing you had waited. Timing matters as much as compatibility. Sometimes you've met the right person, but one or both of you are not yet *ready*, or *whole*. If you don't heal first, you'll bleed on the next person who didn't cut you. For this reason, broken people often build broken homes that raise broken children who perpetuate a broken generation. Wholeness is generational restoration that begins with your healing, not your hoping. So, before praying *for* the right partner, pray to *become* the right partner.

As for a broken partner, it's not your responsibility to fix a broken person. That's between that person and God. Too often, we confuse love with rescue. We mistake empathy for obligation and compassion for calling. However, discernment teaches us that healing is an *invitation*, not an *assignment*.

When we take responsibility for another person's wholeness, we unconsciously assume the role of savior, one already filled by God. We begin to measure our worth by their progress and tie our peace to their healing. Yet, love was never meant to become a form of control. The moment you start carrying what only God can restore, you become weighed down by burdens that were never yours to bear.

Discernment allows you to love wisely. It helps you see where care ends and codependency begins. It says, *"I can walk beside you, but I cannot walk for you."* It recognizes that while you can support someone through their healing journey, you cannot substitute your will for their willingness. Healing requires personal responsibility. If the other person refuses accountability, your efforts become rescue missions rather than redemptive partnerships.

Sometimes, God allows you to witness another person's brokenness not to fix it, but to face your own, including your need to be needed, fear of rejection, or desire to prove your worth through self-sacrifice. Discernment reveals that your job is to *reflect love*, not *replace God*.

Whole love doesn't try to mend people; it mirrors truth. It says, *"I love you enough to step back and let God do what only He can do."* That's not abandonment; that's alignment. It is honoring divine order, recognizing that true healing flows vertically before it can flourish horizontally.

The Power of Love

Love does not break us; it reveals what was already fractured. Heartbreak, rejection, and betrayal often surface wounds we have long avoided. The danger is not in loving. It is in losing ourselves in the process.

Wholeness begins when we allow love to expose what needs healing rather than using it to hide our pain. Love can become a mirror instead of a mask.

God wastes nothing. Even our failures and regrets can become part of our restoration when we bring them into the light. Shame may tell you that you are too broken to love or be loved, but wholeness grows when broken pieces are surrendered, not hidden.

Many people are searching for love while still broken. They believe that if they find the "right" person, everything will finally feel complete. However, relationships cannot repair what identity has not yet restored. Two broken people cannot build a whole relationship. Wholeness must come first.

You are not required to carry everything you uncover here. Let your journal hold the feelings, story or image that arose. You are not required to explain or fix it, only to witness it. The goal is honesty and exploration, not self-interrogation.

3

WHOLENESS: THE EXPRESSION OF OUR BEING

Wholeness begins with identifying who you are *(be)*, not with what you do or have. It is not about being perfect; it is about being aligned. It's when the way of your being matches the truth of your being. In other words, when who you are on the outside reflects who you truly are within. Wholeness is living authentically and purposefully, grounded in worth that is not up for negotiation.

True wholeness means living from the inside out. It is understanding that *being informs doing*. Identity should define activity, not the other way around. Christ embodied this flawlessly. He refused to define Himself by status, success, or others' opinions. He knew who He was and, therefore, didn't need to prove it or have others verify it. When we live from that same awareness, other people's actions, such as their rejection, betrayal, or indifference, no longer diminish our worth. Their behavior reveals their own values, not ours.

Wholeness calls us home. When identity leads, activity can serve; when activity leads, identity starves. If, for instance, our sense of worth rises and falls with a call back or contract secured, then outcomes rather than truth are directing our lives. That's not love. It's dependency dressed in desire.

Definition of Wholeness

In Whole Relationships, wholeness is not a private trophy; it's the ground where healthy love grows. It integrates our three core frameworks:

- **ARC of Self** (**Self-Aware, Self-Respecting, Self-Confident**): Wholeness begins by connecting inward by seeing truth, honoring it, and acting from it.
- **Soul Needs** (**Universal & Unique**): Wholeness deepens as we understand the needs that shape us (truth, love, faith) and the way our purpose, personality, and perspective express them through our talent, traits and time.

- **TORCH of Love (Trust, Openness, Respect, Communication, Humility)**: Wholeness shows up in how we love others – reliable, transparent, honoring, clear, and teachable.

Wholeness is not a mystery. It is alignment between who you are, what you need, and how you love. The journey that follows in this book explores how that alignment develops from the ARC of Self to the discovery of Soul Needs, and finally to the practice of love through the TORCH.

Put simply: Wholeness is the inward integrity that makes outward intimacy safe. **It is when nothing inside you is hiding from the truth anymore.** Your beliefs, values, and behaviors no longer contradict each other; they align. It is alignment lived out, such that what you believe, what you value, and how you live all match.

Beliefs and values are not random preferences. They are shaped by the deeper needs of the soul, which we will explore more fully in Part III. When these needs are understood and honored, alignment becomes possible.

Without alignment, we ask relationships to do what only alignment can do – complete us. However, the miracle of whole love isn't that it completes someone; it calls people to become complete within themselves so they can connect to another soul from fullness, not lack.

Wholeness unfolds in a clear direction. It begins within the self, deepens as we understand the needs of the soul, and ultimately expresses itself in how we love others.

Outsourcing Our Wholeness

We outsource our wholeness when we perform or please to secure validation. It happens when we allow things, circumstances or people to answer the question of who we are. Outsourcing may feel satisfying at first because of the personal acknowledgment, social approval, and tangible rewards create a temporary sense of security. However, the long-term cost often includes anxiety, resentment, and chronic self-betrayal. The reward of being authentic and self-assured, on the other hand, is freedom and integrity, the steady ground of true wholeness.

In business, outsourcing occurs when companies hire external providers to perform tasks that would otherwise be handled internally. It's often done to save time, reduce costs, or increase efficiency, especially when a company wants to scale or grow. In relationships, outsourcing works much the same way. We delegate personal responsibility for our identity. We allow others to manage invaluable emotional processes, such as our self-worth, confidence, and peace. We do it out of need or fear, hoping someone else can give us what we haven't yet learned to provide for ourselves.

The result? We look to relationships for identity, stability or validation that we have not yet secured internally. Instead of connecting from fullness, we attach from lack. When love becomes a solution to emptiness, it quietly becomes pressure. No relationship can carry the weight of completing what only wholeness can integrate.

Many spend years trying to prove their value through achievement, possessions, or relationships, unaware that their worth was never in question. When the relationship ends, the job closes, or the applause fades, the identity fractures because it was anchored to outcomes rather than truth. Here are other examples of what outsourcing looks like:

- **Approval:** "If this relationship works out, then I'm enough."
- **Achievement:** "If I get the role, the deal, the title, then I'm legitimate."
- **Image:** "If I look unbothered and accomplished, then I'm secure."

The problem isn't wanting love or success; it's **assigning others the job of defining your identity.** When, for instance, a partner cheats, withdraws, or simply doesn't choose you, it reveals *their* capacity, character or readiness, not your value. Their behavior belongs to their being and becoming. The same is true for you. Your identity is not up for a vote.

> *"When we outsource our wholeness, we trade authenticity for approval."*

Wholeness lets you tell the truth without collapsing: *"That hurt"* (Openness), *"Here's what I need"* (Communication), *"I will not abandon myself to be accepted by you"* (Respect + Boundaries). That's ARC fueling TORCH.

Wholeness does not ask you to become someone new. It invites you to stop abandoning who you already are. If you noticed yourself recalling times you relied on attention, achievement, or approval to feel whole, pause and explore where that need was first formed. Let the story unfold without censoring it in your journal.

Healing vs. Wholeness

In Chapter 1, we distinguished healing from wholeness. That distinction matters here because outsourcing our identity is often an attempt to heal through attachment. Healing addresses a *wound*. Wholeness addresses a *way* of living. You can be in the healing process (still tender) and still live in alignment (still true). Healing may take time. Wholeness requires integrity.

Think of wholeness as **honest stewardship**: You take the realities of your story seriously without letting them dictate your future. Instead of numbing or "stuffing" pain with productivity or chasing validation for relief, you start metabolizing it with awareness, boundaries, and support.

Wholeness expresses itself in five dimensions:

- **Emotional:** I feel fully without letting feelings dictate my direction.
- **Mental:** I challenge lies with truth and language that honors reality.
- **Physical:** I listen to my body's alarms and build rhythms that regulate.
- **Social:** I choose people who are safe enough to grow with me.
- **Spiritual:** I anchor identity in God's love, not human variability.

Sometimes we avoid healing by constructing identity around **doing** and **having** instead of **being**. Some people hide behind successful careers, titles, wealth, or influence because it feels safer than tending to what hurts. Achievement becomes a costume. Productivity becomes a shield. Influence becomes a mask. However, these externals don't reveal whether someone is healed. They reveal whether someone is *accomplished*.

In my book *The Five Ways We Work*, I explain how our culture glorifies life in reverse:

1. We chase **having** in the form of wealth, status or visibility.
2. We define ourselves by **doing** in performance, productivity and output.
3. We neglect **being** – identity, wholeness, truth.

This reversed order leads to burnout, disconnection, anxiety, and a constant sense of inadequacy because we attempt to build identity from the outside in. Wholeness calls us back to the **inside-out order of being**. It is not about success as proof of stability; it is about alignment as proof of authenticity.

This is why we are often shocked when famous or wealthy people collapse under the weight of internal wounds. Achievement can elevate you, but it cannot stabilize you. Wholeness expresses the healed, integrated self behind the accomplishment, not in place of it.

What is Your Lifestyle Mode?

Being	Doing	Having
• Submissive mode	• Driven mode	• Egocentric mode
• Focused on *"accepting"* and *"allowing"*	• Focused on getting things done, making things happen	• Focused on impressing and/or influencing
• Self-esteem is based on appreciation of life and existence	• Self-esteem is based on achievement and/or approval	• Self-esteem is based on material gain or earnings
• Fear of not being in alignment	• Fear of not being capable or achieving	• Fear of not being worthy

Identity requires a decision: Who are you or who are you becoming? Again, who you are is not about what you do or have done. It's not about what you have or don't have. We are not our title, accomplishments or income. This means having an identity that doesn't collapse without external validation and defining self-worth beyond performance and possessions. This may mean separating who you are from what you've built or established.

Christ as the Model of Wholeness

Jesus is the blueprint for living from truth. He refused the shortcuts of status and spectacle because He knew who He was. He didn't barter identity for influence or trade conviction for safety. His **way of being** – humble, obedient, grounded – matched the **truth of His identity** as the beloved Son of God. That inner certainty produced outward clarity: He said "yes" with purpose and "no" with peace.

If Christ is our model, then wholeness is not stoicism or self-reliance; it is **God-reliance**, an identity rooted in the One who created us. From that place, we can surrender pride (humility), speak truth in love (communication + respect), and trust that provision and protection are not earned by performance but received in alignment.

Jesus' encounter with the woman at the well offers a living picture of wholeness. He did not recoil from her history or require her to fix herself before engaging her. He met her in truth and grace simultaneously. He named what she had hidden, not to shame her, but to free her. In that moment, her fractured story was not ignored or excused; it was integrated. Wholeness begins when what we try to hide is met with truth and grace rather than shame. Thus, wholeness does not deny brokenness. It brings it into the light without fear.

From Doing to Being: The Wholeness Flow

Brokenness often teaches us to perform for belonging. We learn to do in order to be loved by achieving, impressing, fixing or proving. Over time, identity becomes attached to output.

Wholeness reverses that order. It begins with being. When identity is secure, behavior flows from truth rather than striving. We no longer act to earn love; we act from alignment. Doing becomes expression, not desperation.

Wholeness is a flow, a movement that begins internally and expresses itself externally.

1. **Self-Awareness:** *What is true?* (ARC: see the mirror without shame)
2. **Self-Respect:** *How will I honor it?* (Boundaries, standards, dignity)
3. **Self-Confidence:** *How will I act from it?* (Courageous choices aligned with identity)
4. **Soul Needs:** *What must be nourished?* (Universal: truth, love, faith; Unique: talent, traits, time)
5. **TORCH:** *How will this love show up?* (Trustworthy, Open, Reverent, Clear, Humble)

When these inner steps are rushed or skipped, relationships become places from which we try to **extract** (validation, certainty, safety, relief) instead of places where we **exchange** (mutuality, service, growth) whole love. When they are honored, love becomes a shared practice of truth rather than a shared performance of fear.

Wholeness is a lifestyle, not a single achievement**. It's a daily practice**, a lived rhythm. It unfolds in simple phases:

Awareness → Acceptance → Alignment → Action

If this feels heavy, that's understandable. Awareness often brings weight before it brings clarity.

Courage, Not Control

Brokenness often expresses itself through control. When safety feels uncertain, we try to manage outcomes, regulate other people's responses, or reduce risk by tightening our grip. Control becomes the counterfeit of safety. It soothes anxiety temporarily but erodes trust over time.

Courage is different. Courage does not manage people; it reveals truth. It is the willingness to be seen and to speak honestly, even when the outcome isn't guaranteed. Courage says:

- **To myself:** I won't betray who I am to belong.
- **To you:** I will be clear and kind, even if clarity costs me closeness.
- **To God:** I will trust Your leading over their approval.

It takes courage to face the truth without weaponizing it. When we are aligned with truth, we no longer manipulate for security or shrink for acceptance. We stand grounded in who we are, trusting that what is truly meant for us will not require self-abandonment.

Psychologically, this is what creates emotional safety. Research consistently shows that relationships thrive not because conflict disappears, but because partners feel safe enough to be honest about their needs, fears, and flaws (Gottman & Silver 2015). Emotional safety, not perfection, allows love to thrive. Perfection is impossible, but presence is attainable. Wholeness replaces performance with presence and fear with alignment.

If you recognize ways you've avoided pain through productivity, relationships or performance, pause here and write about what you've been trying not to feel.

Whole Relationships Modules

Wholeness unfolds directionally. It begins with connection to the self, deepens through commitment to growth, clarifies through understanding soul needs, and matures through connection and commitment to others.

*In Part II, you will develop **connection to self** through the ARC of Self, learning awareness, respect, and confidence, and then sustain it through a **commitment to yourself**.

*In Part III, you will explore the Soul Needs that shape your beliefs, values, and behaviors.

*In Part IV, you will practice **connection to others** through the TORCH of Love.

*In Part V, you will examine what **commitment to others** requires for love to endure.

Each module builds on the one before it, guiding you from self-connection to soul clarity to healthy, whole relationships. You do not move forward by mastering everything at once, but by growing in sequence.

Wholeness begins with honest awareness of your internal patterns. To uncover your patterns that could be inhibiting your wholeness, take "**The Whole Relationship Self-Assessment**" (see **Appendix B**) to determine how healed or whole you are.

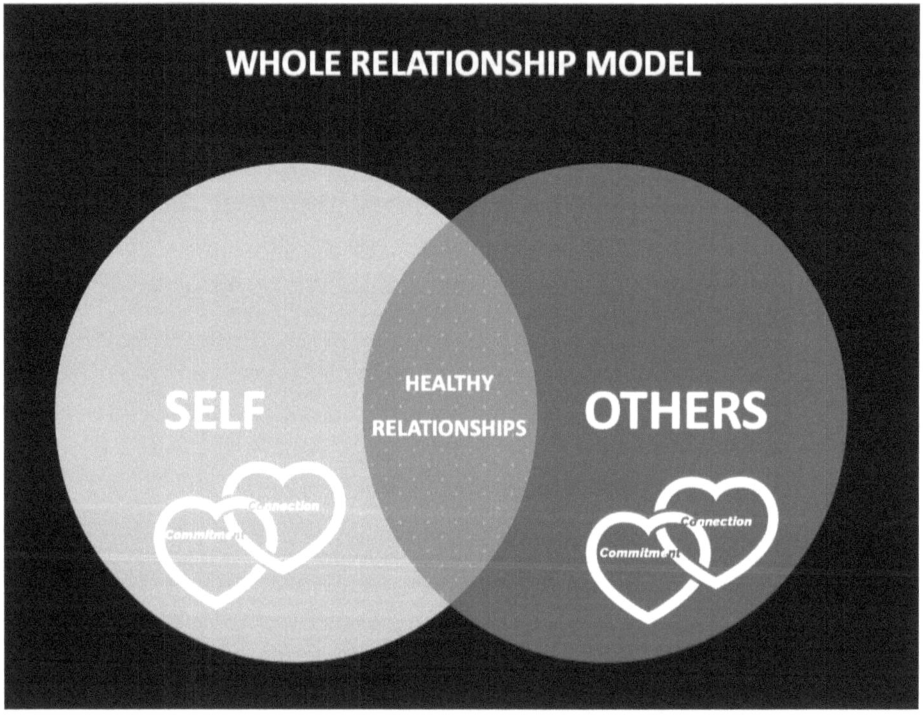

The model below illustrates how connection with self and connection with others intersect to form healthy relationships. The modules you will explore build upon this foundation.

PART I REVIEW: FROM BROKENNESS TO WHOLENESS

By now, you've explored the landscape of brokenness, including how it forms, hides, and speaks. You've also examined the journey toward wholeness, which is less about perfection and more about reclaiming the truth of who you are.

Brokenness distorts our identity, shaping lies we unknowingly believe about ourselves and the world:

- *"I am not enough."*
- *"Love must be earned."*
- *"My feelings are a burden."*
- *"Control keeps me safe."*
- *"If people knew the real me, they would leave."*

These lies don't just live in the mind; they settle into habits, choices, relationships, and even the way we speak to ourselves. They become a way of surviving but not a way of living.

Wholeness, on the other hand, is the steady reclaiming of truth:

- *"I am inherently worthy."*
- *"Love is expressed, not negotiated."*
- *"My emotions are intelligent messengers."*
- *"I can trust wisely without abandoning myself."*
- *"The right people embrace the real me."*

Wholeness doesn't erase your past; it restores your power. It doesn't erase your wounds; it teaches you how to handle them with wisdom. It doesn't erase your humanity; it reveals your divinity.

The movement from brokenness to wholeness is not a straight line. It is a practice of telling the truth, choosing awareness, setting boundaries, listening inward, and learning how to love without losing yourself. The wholeness flow is simple:

1. See the truth.
2. Honor the truth.
3. Live the truth.

As you move into Part II, keep this in mind:

Brokenness teaches you to fear yourself. Wholeness teaches you to trust yourself.

Self-awareness is where wholeness begins because it opens the door to every other aspect of whole relationships, especially when conflict arises. This is where your journey deepens.

Before beginning Part II, review the affirmations that support emotional and spiritual alignment in **Appendix E** *along with the related prompts to process emotional healing and safety in* **Appendix F**. *You are not meant to carry all of this internally.*

PART II

THE JOURNEY WITHIN

Connecting and Committing to Self

4

AWARENESS: THE FOUNDATION OF SELF-CONNECTION

Before we can love another person well, we must first learn to live honestly within ourselves. The hardest person to be honest with is often ourselves, though. We may fight hard to maintain the identity we have adopted. To insulate our pain or uphold our identity, we create stories – small, believable lies that help us survive what we do not yet know how to face. This is self-deception: rationalizing behavior, minimizing truth, or disguising insecurity as confidence.

The TEA

Every behavior begins as a *belief* about ourselves, others, and/or the world. Thus, the misconceptions we live by are often born in the space between our thoughts, emotions, and actions, a cycle known as the TEA Process. This simple framework helps us see how our inner world shapes the way we show up in relationships.

Self-awareness begins when we are willing to look beneath the story and trace what is actually happening inside us. The **TEA Process** reminds us that every external action begins as an internal belief:

T – Thoughts → E – Emotions → A – Actions

Our **thoughts** shape our **emotions**, and our emotions drive our **actions**.

For example, when a thought is rooted in fear, shame or scarcity, it produces anxiety, anger or defensiveness. Those emotions then express themselves through avoidance, control or withdrawal. Over time, this broken pattern reinforces the very disconnection we are trying to avoid.

When brokenness distorts our thinking, we begin to live out lies as if they were truth. These are some examples of both distorted beliefs we adopt in brokenness and the truths we believe in wholeness:

Brokenness

- **Lie**: "I have to be perfect."
- **Lie**: "I am not enough."
- **Lie**: "I'm too damaged to be loved."
- **Lie**: "It's safer not to feel anything."

Wholeness

- **Truth**: "My past does not define me."
- **Truth**: "I am worthy of love and respect."
- **Truth**: "I heal by being honest with myself first."
- **Truth**: "My value is rooted in who I am, not what I produce."

The good news is that the cycle can be interrupted. By pausing to examine our thoughts before we react, we invite awareness into the process. Changing a thought grounded in a lie (e.g. "They're going to leave," or "I have to prove my worth") shifts the emotional tone and opens new behavioral choices. Awareness becomes the first step toward wholeness.

Simply naming what you are feeling can calm the emotion itself, acting as a "name it to tame it" method. When you pause and say, "I feel angry," "I feel afraid," or "I feel hurt," the feeling begins to lose some of its intensity. Naming an emotion creates a small space between the feeling and your reaction, literally shifting your brain activity from an emotional response to a more rational one. In that space, awareness grows. You regain the ability to think clearly, respond wisely, and choose your next action rather than being driven by the emotion in the moment.

Self-awareness, then, is self-honesty, not self-criticism. It asks: *What am I thinking right now? What emotion is that producing? How is it shaping the way I'm showing up?* When we learn to answer those questions with compassion and curiosity, self-deception loses its power, and self-connection begins. Healing begins when we confront the lie at the level of thought, allowing truth to transform how we feel and ultimately how we love.

This readiness to honor truth is what carries self-awareness into wholeness, which involves being perfectly ready to acknowledge and respond to the truth – both yours and other people's. Again, it doesn't mean you're perfect. In fact, the opposite is true. It means you're ready to deal with your imperfection in a truthful manner and do so on a routine basis.

The Mirror of Truth

Sometimes we think the people we are involved with are the problem, but they may actually be the mirror, reflecting our own brokenness. So, instead of complaining about or blaming them, we can ask ourselves: What is this situation trying to teach me or show me about me? As Pastor Dale Bonner observed, the broken can become "masters at mending" when they glean lessons from negative situations.[1]

I once dated a man named Thomas for almost two years. He often canceled plans or told me he already had something else scheduled with family or friends. He seemed to love my affirmation and validation of his looks and talent, yet he never offered the same in return.

I later learned he had a *dismissive-avoidant attachment style*, a pattern shaped by early emotional neglect, leading him to equate closeness with danger and independence with safety. It wasn't that he didn't care; he simply lacked the capacity to care deeply. His wounded inner child had built a wall to protect him from emotional intimacy. Dismissive-avoidant attachment is one of the primary patterns described in attachment theory, first identified by psychologists John Bowlby and Mary Ainsworth.

At the time, I didn't have the clinical language to describe his behavior, but I knew something was deeply wrong. I thought the problem was just him. What I didn't expect was to realize that everything his behavior triggered in me was a mirror of my own brokenness, my wounded inner child. I was *overfunctioning*, initiating most of the communication and trying to hold the relationship together because I was still trying to earn love, just as I had in childhood. I hadn't yet faced my fear of abandonment, my struggle to set boundaries or my tendency to shrink my needs when I met resistance.

> ***"Awareness begins when we stop blaming the mirror and start tending to the reflection."***

If this example mirrors a relationship in your life, pause and take this reflection to your journal. Write from the part of you that may have learned to overfunction, shrink or earn love.

---

1 Dale Bonner, sermon delivered at Word of Faith Church, Austell, GA, November 5, 2025.

What the Mirror Reveals

We often try to *outsource our wholeness*, seeking people who make us feel complete, rather than taking responsibility for healing our own wounds. Some relationships exist to trigger the self-work we've ignored, inviting us to find our peace, worth, and safety within.

When you don't know what you need, you'll either demand too much or settle for too little. It's our responsibility to create a personal container where love can grow. Only then can we invite a partner to meet needs like affection, affirmation, and being heard.

An avoidant partner's silence, distance or withdrawal can serve as a mirror, not because their behavior is your fault, but because it stirs what's already inside: unhealed fears of abandonment, rejection, or not being enough.

When you feel triggered by someone's withdrawal, it's often your *inner child* responding, the one who learned that love might mean being overlooked or emotionally starved. The shrinking, the apologizing, the overexplaining, the longing, they're not really about the other person. They're your nervous system's way of trying to regulate pain. However, here's the truth:

You are worthy of love, even if someone else is not giving it.

God's message may be this: stop outsourcing your worth to someone else's availability or affection. Reclaim that power. Let the little girl inside you know she is safe now and that you, the adult, will protect, love, and choose her. From that grounded place, you can finally ask:

"Does this relationship actually deserve me?"

(Is this relationship honoring who I am or costing me who I am?)

Ask this not from pride, but from clarity garnered from self-awareness.

Relational pain can also be a sacred invitation back to *you*. The love you were always seeking in someone else may be the one you're now learning to give to yourself. For instance:

Someone's silence is not proof that I'm unlovable. It's a mirror reflecting the part of me that still believes I have to earn love, fix others or chase connection to feel safe.

This isn't about blame, neither his nor yours. It's about seeing pain as sacred information. When you heal what it reveals, the panic fades, and you stop settling for relationships that keep re-injuring the same wound. Remember this:

Awareness begins when we stop blaming the mirror and start tending to the reflection.

Balance as a Mirror of Wholeness

One of the clearest indicators of brokenness is imbalance. When one area of life consistently dominates the others, something is out of alignment. Being whole does not mean excelling at everything equally, but it does mean honoring every essential part of your life, including health, home life, work, and relationships.

Many people mistake imbalance for dedication. Overworking is praised as ambition. Emotional neglect is reframed as independence. Physical depletion is dismissed as the cost of success. Yet these patterns are not signs of wholeness; they are often compensations for unmet needs elsewhere.

Self-awareness reveals imbalance through patterns. If your identity is wrapped entirely in productivity, your worth may feel conditional. If your relationships thrive while your body deteriorates, you may be sacrificing sustainability for connection. If your inner world is rich but your outer life is in disarray, avoidance may be masquerading as spirituality.

Wholeness is expressed through balance, not perfection. A whole life makes room for care of the heart, maintenance of one's world, stewardship of the body, and meaningful work. When any one of these consistently consumes the others, it signals not strength, but fragmentation.

Awareness invites an honest question: *Where am I overinvested, and what am I neglecting?* The answer is not meant to shame you, but to show you where healing and realignment are needed.

In later chapters, we will explore how commitment becomes lived alignment, not through pressure, but through daily rhythms that honor your whole life.

Awareness grows through repetition, not revelation. If you notice yourself wanting to move quickly toward solutions, pause. The workbook includes simple awareness practices meant to slow reactivity and strengthen self-connection. Use them as often as needed; this work is cyclical, not linear. In this book, go to ***Appendix E*** *for self-awareness affirmations and* ***Appendix F*** *for related prompts necessary to reinforce this lesson.*

5

RESPECT: HONORING YOUR DIVINE DESIGN

Respect is the second movement of the ARC of Self. Awareness reveals truth. Respect decides what we will do with it. I learned that lesson the hard way.

I once received a text from my ex, Peter, inviting me to a house party. I was excited because I never truly received closure when our six-month relationship ended. What I did not realize until shortly after I arrived was that he now shared that house with his new girlfriend and her children.

There I was, trying to prove myself again. I was determined that I would not let him see me sweat. I told myself I was unbothered. I smiled. I stayed. I did not realize that the cost of protecting my ego was the truth: he was unworthy of my time and attention, and I had known that before I arrived. That night only confirmed it.

Awareness was present. Respect was not. Instead of honoring what I saw clearly, I chose to play along. I stuffed my emotions rather than face them. I remained in an environment that diminished me because I did not yet believe that leaving would honor me.

This had been the second time in my dating life that I stayed in a situation where a man invited multiple women to an event to boost his ego. The pattern was no longer accidental. It was instructional.

Respect requires more than recognizing truth. It requires protecting it. In the ARC of Self, awareness exposes truth, but respect protects it. Without respect, awareness becomes information without transformation. We may see clearly and still stay. We may recognize red flags and still rationalize them. Respect is where integrity begins.

After the situation with Peter, I realized I had been "stuffing" my emotions, pushing down hurt and confusion instead of facing them, but I didn't even realize it. "Stuffing emotions" means suppressing or burying feelings rather than processing them – denying pain rather than allowing healing. I had mastered this as a form of self-protection, but it only deepened my disconnection from myself. I wasn't standing up for the inner child who once felt like the least favorite growing up. I had learned how to survive for so long without love from my primary caregiver that this environment, a party for my ex and his girlfriend, didn't even shake me. I was numb to humiliation because the pain of rejection had become familiar.

True *respect* begins with ourselves, not others. To respect someone or something is to honor them in posture and practice. This can take two forms: **positional respect** or **relational respect.** Positional respect means we honor someone's *authority or role*. Relational respect means we honor the person's *heart* – their feelings, expectations, and emotional boundaries.

Self-respect is the act of honoring your own needs, values, and dignity once awareness has exposed them. Respecting yourself is just as important, if not more so, than respecting others. It begins when you recognize your God-given worth and refuse to let others define it for you.

Self-worth doesn't come from other people. It is inherent, *given by God* at birth. Everyone has worth. The challenge is learning to honor it in yourself without needing reassurance or comparison.

Love Without Respect

Many people confuse being *chosen* with being *honored.* Just because someone chooses you doesn't mean they respect you, and just because someone says they love you doesn't mean they value you. Being *chosen* may simply mean you meet a need for comfort, companionship or convenience in that moment. Being *respected*, however, means your worth, boundaries, and individuality are seen and protected.

Some people will "choose" you for how you make them feel, not for who you are. They may love your light but still disregard your limits. They may enjoy your loyalty but neglect your voice.

Love without respect becomes ownership. Respect without love becomes distance. True partnership requires both. That's why respect is the test of love's maturity. Real love doesn't ask you to shrink, perform, or tolerate what violates your peace. It honors who you are while protecting what you value.

So, when someone says, *"I love you,"* ask yourself, *"Do they respect me?"* because where respect ends, love begins to decay.

In ARC terms, respect is the internal guardrail that prevents awareness from collapsing into self-betrayal. You may be aware that something feels wrong.

Respect determines whether you tolerate it.

> *"Respect is love's proof."*

Key Self-Respect Takeaways:

- *Being chosen doesn't equal being cherished.*
- *Being loved doesn't guarantee being respected.*
- *Respect is love's proof.*

Knowing Your Value

When you respect yourself, you stop auditioning for spaces that dishonor you. You no longer settle for attention that costs your peace or validation that diminishes your value. Respect becomes the quiet boundary that says: *"I will not abandon myself to be accepted by you."*

Your divine design already holds value. The lesson is not to earn it, but to remember it. Think of your love as something worth earning, not as a prize to hoard but as a reflection of your own self-worth. When you know your value, you stop giving yourself away cheaply. Yet, valuing yourself doesn't mean you are *more valuable* than your partner. It means you both recognize each other's worth and meet each other in mutual honor. Love loses its power when one person's value is inflated at the expense of the other's dignity.

*Go to **Appendix E** for affirmations (e.g. Mirror of Awareness) and **Appendix F** for related prompts necessary to reinforce this lesson.*

Accountability: Self-Respect in Action

Accountability is self-respect in motion. It is how respect expresses itself behaviorally. It is neither self-blame nor self-protection. It is the ability to take responsibility for your words, actions, and impact without collapsing into shame or hardening into defensiveness. When self-respect is healthy, accountability becomes possible. You can acknowledge where you were wrong without losing your sense of worth, and you can receive correction without interpreting it as rejection.

Brokenness often distorts accountability in one of two ways. Some people take responsibility for everything, apologizing reflexively and absorbing blame that is not theirs. Others rarely take responsibility at all, avoiding reflection and deflecting fault to preserve control. Both patterns reflect a fractured relationship with self-respect. Brokenness often distorts accountability in two opposite directions:

- **Over-accountable**:
    - Chronic apologizing
    - Taking responsibility for others' emotions
    - Confusing humility with self-erasure
- **Under-accountable**:
    - Chronic defensiveness
    - Externalizing blame
    - Confusing confidence with infallibility

Wholeness restores balance, allowing accountability to function as growth, not punishment. Healthy accountability fosters growth and wholeness by:

- Taking responsibility for your words, actions, and impact
- Allowing correction without collapse or defensiveness
- Building trust through consistency and consideration
- Setting boundaries that honor your value and needs

When self-respect is intact, you can acknowledge where you were wrong without collapsing into shame, and you can receive correction without interpreting it as rejection.

Setting Boundaries and Life Rules

True respect doesn't stop at self-worth; it extends into how you *live it out*. In the ARC of Self, boundaries are the behavioral expression of respect. They are how alignment becomes visible. Self-respect without boundaries is like a home without walls. It may have beauty, but it has no protection. Boundaries are how you guard what you've learned to value in yourself. They define the space where peace, dignity, and love can thrive.

A boundary is a personal rule you set for yourself, not for others. It governs how you choose to operate, not how you attempt to control or direct others. In this sense, boundaries are not the same as rules imposed on others. For example, saying, "Don't call me after 10 o'clock" is a rule. Saying, "I don't answer calls after 10 p.m." is a boundary.

Similarly, a standard is something you live by, not something you impose on others. Therefore, expectations are not the same as standards. For instance, believing that a man should always drive is an expectation, placing a specific demand on someone's behavior that can lead to disappointment or frustration if it's not met. A standard, on the other hand, reflects your own values and choices. For example, you might have a standard of only associating with men who are considerate and willing to share responsibilities.

Expectations are outward-facing, focused on what you want others to do. **Standards** are inward-facing, focused on what you choose to accept or align yourself with.

Just as rules are outward attempts to control others' behavior ("Don't call me after 10"), expectations also focus on what others should do ("A man should always drive"). Meanwhile, boundaries and standards are inward-facing, practical expressions of self-respect. They're about how you choose to live and what you will or won't accept or engage with:

- A **boundary** says, "I don't answer calls after 10." It's about your own action or limit, not forcing someone else to behave a certain way.
- A **standard** says, "I only associate with people who are considerate." It's about your criteria for who you allow into your life, not a demand placed on a specific person.

You can think of:

- **Rule vs. Boundary** = outward vs. inward control of behavior
- **Expectation vs. Standard** = outward vs. inward values and choices

Boundaries and standards are the outer fences of self-respect. They don't restrict love; they protect it. They help ensure that what you build with others reflects the value God already placed within you.

Rules are not punishment, rigidity or control. They are containers that make wholeness sustainable. In whole relationships, we develop **life rules** for ourselves, not others. Here is how it breaks down:

- Boundaries say *no*
- Rules say *how*
- Self-respect sustains both

Wholeness is not sustained by intention alone; it requires structure that supports alignment over time. This is where personal life rules become essential. A rule of life is not about control, rigidity, or spiritual performance. It is about creating conditions where truth, obedience, and integrity are easier to choose than avoidance, fear, or comfort. I became aware of this in my own life through recurring frustration with procrastination, delaying things I knew were urgent or important, not because I didn't care, but because perfectionism made beginning feel risky. The fear of producing something imperfect quietly eroded my self-respect, turning delay into a form of self-protection rather than discipline. Naming that pattern revealed a deeper through-line: choosing comfort over obedience was interfering with both my faith and fulfillment. In response, I established a few simple life rules to support alignment, not as standards to be copied, but as personal guardrails that help me act with clarity rather than hesitation. In a whole relationship lifestyle, rules are not restrictions placed on life; they are conditions that protect self-respect and make faithful, consistent living possible.

Life rules are deeply personal and often deceptively simple. For some, a rule may sound like pausing before responding when emotions rise or committing to begin important tasks before seeking distraction or validation. For others, it may involve asking a single clarifying question when fear or impulsivity takes over or building in brief moments of reflection that reconnect intention to action. The form of the rule matters less than its purpose: **to support alignment when old patterns would otherwise lead**.

> *"When you have no boundaries, you get no respect."*

Boundaries are not walls; they are evidence. They reveal how you value yourself and teach others how to value you as well. Life rules are personal supports for alignment, designed to protect what matters most. When you begin to honor your limits, you stop negotiating your worth through availability or approval. This is where self-respect becomes visible, not just internal. Once respect is embodied, confidence no longer needs to be manufactured. It emerges naturally from alignment.

Setting boundaries and life rules often brings up fear, guilt or self-doubt. If that's true for you, you're not failing; you're becoming aware. The workbook provides boundary-language and life rules exercises, along with examples, to help you practice clarity without over-explaining or self-betrayal. Let it support you here in developing these necessary skills.

Respect stabilizes identity, but it does not complete the ARC. Once you see truth and honor it, you must act from it. That movement requires confidence, the courage to live visibly from what you know. That is where we turn next.

6

CONFIDENCE: BELIEVING IN YOUR BECOMING

Confidence grows out of self-respect, not perfection. It is not an attitude or a performance; it is a settled trust in your ability to handle challenges and remain anchored in who you are. It expresses itself through courageous truth-telling – verbally and nonverbally – without apology or self-erasure.

If awareness allows you to see clearly and respect teaches you to honor what you see, confidence requires you to live from it. It is integrity in motion. It is the willingness to act on what you know, even when the outcome is uncertain.

True confidence has little to do with image or control and everything to do with *integrity*, the courage to show up honestly as you are, not as you think you should be. It is the quiet assurance that your worth is not determined by flawless performance but by faithful presence.

Confidence begins with trust. To be confident is to trust your own judgment, abilities, and limitations. With God's guidance, you are equipped to meet both success and struggle with steadiness. Self-confidence involves accepting both your strengths and your limits without shame. You can make mistakes and still remain whole.

Confidence in wholeness is not self-exaltation; it is settled identity. Christ did not prove Himself; He revealed Himself. In the same way, confidence does not demand validation. It expresses alignment.

Confidence becomes clear in ordinary moments:

- Saying no without apology
- Staying present without shrinking
- Remaining steady when misunderstood
- Refusing to perform for acceptance

While self-esteem measures how you feel about yourself, confidence reflects how you trust yourself: how you show up in action, conversation, and commitment. Confidence does not wait for certainty; it moves with faith.

When we cultivate confidence, we no longer hide behind perfectionism, pride, or passivity. We practice courageous honesty – first with ourselves and then with others, allowing God to shape our becoming through every faithful step we take.

Courage to Be Seen

I've often told myself I'm just picky when it comes to romantic relationships or that I'm simply waiting on the Lord to send the "right" man, but the truth runs deeper: I'm not picky; I'm scared.

I'm afraid of being exposed and having my imperfections, fears, and wounds seen and possibly rejected. So rather than risk vulnerability, I retreat. I withdraw into silence or distance, forcing others to work their way through an emotional maze just to reach me. I call it being "wise," but really, it's fear in disguise.

I've mislabeled my emotional avoidance as high standards or low tolerance for nonsense. In reality, I've been emotionally malnourished. I've mistaken the hunger for connection as a call to be selective, when in truth, I've been avoiding the risk of intimacy. I've romanticized the idea of being pursued, not because I want real love, but because I want to feel worthy without having to be vulnerable. That's not love, that's craving worship.

Worship gives me admiration without requiring exposure. Love, on the other hand, demands that I be seen.

Love calls for openness, presence, and mutual effort. Validation only requires that I look good from a distance. When I expect someone to read my silence, guess my triggers, or chase after my withdrawal, I'm not inviting connection; I'm testing people's endurance. That's not a boundary. That's an obstacle course, and emotional intimacy can't grow in a maze.

If I say I want someone who is consistent, emotionally available, and capable of showing up for love, then I have to ask: am I those things myself?

Journaling the traits I say I desire in a partner and then cross-referencing them with my own actions is a mirror I need to look into. If I want consistency, am I consistent? If I value emotional openness, am I practicing it in my own life? If I want unconditional love and acceptance, am I loving and accepting myself unconditionally?

This isn't about self-condemnation; it's about alignment. My standards aren't too high; my self-awareness has been too low. I've said I'm waiting on God's timing, but truthfully, I've been using that as a way to delay doing the hard, sacred work of emotional growth.

Love doesn't just arrive. It meets you where you're willing to be honest, and I can't keep expecting someone to meet me in places I'm not even willing to go myself.

Vulnerability: The Pathway to Reciprocity

Vulnerability isn't weakness; it's a sacred filter. When you allow yourself to be open and emotionally transparent, you don't lose power; you *gain clarity.* Vulnerability reveals what's real. **It is a soul truth that awakens soul truth in another.**

If I'm dealing with someone and I express that I was thinking about him, the right man will be encouraged by that openness. My honesty empowers him to feel safe enough to express his own feelings. That's emotional reciprocity in motion.

If he's not the right one? My vulnerability still serves me. His indifference or lack of response will reveal that truth faster than any guessing game ever could. Vulnerability doesn't just connect; it *discerns.* Remember: *Silence is also a response.*

It's the same for men. When a man shares openly with a woman, the right woman will mirror that openness. She will feel honored, not burdened. However, if she's emotionally unavailable or disinterested, his vulnerability will expose that, too. Either way, honesty gives clarity.

Vulnerability never works against you. It works *for* you. It calls forth truth in the other person and saves you from wasting time and emotional energy on pretense.

Emotional shields, such as walls, withdrawal, avoidance, may protect us from rejection, but they also block the intimacy we long for. It's a paradox: the very armor we use for protection often becomes the barrier that keeps love out.

When we guard too tightly against pain, we also guard against joy, trust, and connection. Vulnerability is not recklessness; it's discernment in motion. It's saying, "I'm willing to be seen, even if it means I might be hurt, because truth is safer than illusion."

Handling Rejection

Rejection is one of the most powerful forces capable of shaking or even shattering self-confidence. Whether rejection comes *indirectly* through silence, avoidance or ghosting, or *directly* through being fired, dismissed or left, the instinctive response is often to turn inward and make it mean something is wrong with us. We begin to question our value, desirability, or worth.

Yet rejection does not automatically mean you are lacking. Often, it simply means that a person, place, or opportunity is not aligned with you. At times, rejection functions as divine protection or redirection, guiding you away from what is not for you and toward what is. When you allow someone else's rejection to define your worth, you surrender your power to their perception rather than remaining anchored in your own value.

Rejection can be especially destabilizing when it comes from those we loved or depended on most, particularly in childhood, before our sense of self was fully formed. Parents, caretakers, or authority figures who were wounded themselves may have withheld affirmation, distorted truth, or projected their own pain onto you. In doing so, they did not reveal your worth; they revealed their brokenness. That early rejection can linger, quietly shaping self-doubt and undermining confidence long into adulthood.

Still, your story does not end there. You can reclaim your power by grounding your confidence in what cannot be taken from you: your inherent, God-given value. You were created and formed by God with intention. You are here because you matter to Him, not because others approved of you.

Scripture reminds us that even Jesus was rejected by His own people, despite expressing unconditional love, divine wisdom, and unmatched integrity. His rejection did not diminish His identity nor did misunderstanding weaken His confidence. He remained anchored in who He was and whose He was. His life reminds us that approval is not something we can earn from people who are determined to misunderstand or oppose us. Confidence grows when identity is rooted beyond public opinion.

At the same time, not all rejection is unjust. There are moments when rejection invites honest self-reflection. While people can certainly be unfair, abusive or judgmental, repeated feedback from different sources may signal something we need to examine. Confidence does not require or involve defensiveness. Healthy confidence allows us to listen, assess, and take responsibility where growth is needed.

When warranted, this reflection may also reveal the impact of our behavior on others. If we have caused harm while operating from brokenness, healing requires more than insight; it requires repair. Addressing the issue within ourselves is only the beginning. True confidence makes room for accountability, growth, and restoration without collapsing into shame.

Confidence, then, is not the absence of rejection. It is the ability to face rejection without losing yourself, to discern truth without self-betrayal, and to remain grounded in your worth while continuing to grow.

> *"Confidence is not self-exaltation. It's settled identity."*

Confidence in Becoming

Confidence invites authenticity; vulnerability makes it visible.

When we trust ourselves, we no longer need to control every outcome or manage every impression. We can let others see us, not because we're flawless but because we're faithful. Confidence gives us the courage to tell the truth about who we are and what we need, even when it feels risky.

Real confidence doesn't say, *"I have it all together."* It says, *"Even when I fall apart, I still belong to God, and I can face myself with honesty and grace."*

This is where confidence and vulnerability meet: in the sacred space where you stop performing and start *becoming*.

---

*Go to **Appendix E** for self-confidence affirmations and **Appendix F** for related prompts necessary to reinforce this lesson.*

Confidence stabilizes identity, but stability must be sustained. Seeing truth and acting from it are not enough if you abandon yourself when pressure rises. The final movement of the journey within is commitment, the decision to remain faithful to the person you are becoming.

7

COMMITTING TO YOURSELF

Commitment to yourself is not about self-obsession; it is about self-integrity. It is the decision to remain loyal to the truth you have already seen, honored, and begun to live. Many people are aware. Some learn to respect what they see. Fewer remain committed when honoring that truth becomes inconvenient.

Connection to self begins the healing, wholeness journey, but commitment to self sustains it.

Through **Awareness**, you learned to see yourself clearly.

Through **Respect**, you learned to honor what you found.

Through **Confidence**, you learned to stand in that truth with courage.

Commitment is the next step, where insight turns into integrity, and identity becomes consistency.

Confidence gives you the courage to tell the truth about who you are and what you need, even when it feels risky. Commitment shows that you value those truths enough to protect and practice them. It is keeping the promises you make to yourself. It is choosing behaviors that align with your worth, especially when no one is watching.

Connection helps you *understand* yourself; commitment teaches you to *trust* yourself. When you commit to your well-being, growth, and goals, you affirm that your needs are sacred, not selfish. This is where self-connection becomes self-partnership. It's where awareness becomes accountability, respect becomes standards, and confidence becomes character.

Commitment to self is the practice of making and keeping promises to yourself. If you do not commit to yourself, you will continually seek reassurance from others to stabilize what you have not secured within.

As Scripture reminds us, "Let your 'Yes' be yes and your 'No' be no" (Matthew 5:37). Commitment begins with congruence.

The Cost of Broken Commitments

Our greatest fear in relationships is often betrayal, or cheating, when someone breaks their commitment to us. Some may think because they aren't officially married yet that cheating doesn't matter as much or maybe at all. However, cheating always matters, whether you're dating, engaged, or married because it represents more than just physical infidelity. It's a fracture of *trust, respect, and integrity.*

Commitment isn't defined by rings, titles, or paperwork. It's defined by *honor*, keeping your word even when emotions change, and respecting the person who trusted you enough to give you access to their heart.

If you're in a relationship and planning a future together, stepping outside of that promise isn't just a mistake; it's a betrayal. If you're not ready to be loyal, you're not ready to be in a relationship. Here's the truth we often overlook: **We betray ourselves far more often than anyone else ever could.**

Awareness reveals the truth, but it does not sustain change. In previous chapters, you may have recognized patterns of imbalance, areas where one part of your life has been carrying the weight of the whole. That recognition is not an indictment; it is information. Seeing where you are overextended or undernourished is the beginning of wholeness, not the end of it. Commitment is what follows awareness. It is the decision to respond to what you now see with care rather than criticism, intention rather than impulse. To commit to yourself is to begin restoring balance through daily choices that honor your whole life.

Breaking commitment to self can look like:

- Having an imbalanced life
- Making promises you don't keep
- Ignoring your intuition to please others
- Staying silent when your soul needs to speak
- Sacrificing your peace to earn someone's approval

These forms of *self-betrayal* might not leave visible scars, but they quietly erode self-trust, the foundation of every healthy relationship.

Why Commitment to Self Matters

Just as infidelity shatters the bond of trust in a relationship, neglecting your promises to yourself fractures your inner integrity. Rebuilding that trust requires patience, compassion, and consistency.

When you keep your word to yourself, you begin to heal that fracture.

- **It builds self-trust and confidence.** Following through on your commitments shows you that your word has weight — not just to others, but to you.
- **It boosts self-esteem.** It demonstrates that your needs and goals matter, strengthening your sense of worth.
- **It promotes personal growth.** Commitment keeps you aligned with your vision, turning potential into progress.
- **It fosters self-compassion.** You learn to encourage rather than criticize yourself through challenges.
- **It increases control over your life.** By honoring your word, you reclaim authorship of your own story.

Keeping your commitments to yourself isn't selfish; it's *sacred stewardship.* It's saying, "I am as worthy of loyalty as anyone I love." The more you practice self-loyalty, the more integrity flows into every relationship around you. Because when you stop cheating yourself, you stop accepting half-truths from others.

Awareness reveals the pattern, self-respect names what must change, and self-confidence supports belief in that change. However, commitment is where transformation actually begins. Many people believe commitment is about resolve or discipline, yet lasting change requires something far more practical. To commit to yourself is to retrain your inner world, not just make a decision about your outer one.

Changing Behavior

Commitment isn't a feeling. It's a neurological agreement you keep practicing. In other words, your brain "agrees" with what you repeatedly practice. Over time, it treats that pattern as truth, and it organizes your thoughts, emotions, and actions around it. Real change, then, is not a matter of motivation or willpower, but a neurological skill. The brain is designed to favor predictability over novelty because what is familiar feels safe. Whatever you repeatedly think, feel, or do becomes a well-worn neural pathway that is efficient, automatic, and comfortable for your nervous system. This is why real change requires more than good intentions. To create new habits and patterns, you must deliberately train your brain in new ways:

- **New thoughts practiced on purpose**, even when the old ones feel more natural

- **New emotional states sustained long enough** for your nervous system to recognize them as safe and familiar
- **New actions repeated consistently** until the brain no longer interprets them as a threat

The moment you stop merely hoping for a different future and begin actively rehearsing it through your thoughts, emotions, and actions, your brain begins to adapt. At first, resistance is normal. Discomfort doesn't mean you're doing something wrong, though. It means your brain is leaving the familiar.

With repetition and patience, the unfamiliar becomes familiar, and once that happens, your brain has no choice but to reorganize itself around the new pattern. Change, then, is not something you hope or wait for; it's something you practice until it becomes who you are.

When commitment is practiced this way, it stops being exhausting and starts becoming embodied. What once felt forced becomes familiar, and what once required effort becomes identity. This is how self-connection deepens, not through intensity but through consistency. Sustaining commitment without pressure or perfectionism requires more than discipline; it requires tenderness. Many of the patterns we are trying to change were formed in seasons when we did not feel protected, guided, or emotionally safe. To commit to yourself fully, you must learn not only how to change your behavior, but how to care for the part of you that learned those patterns in the first place.

Re-Parenting Yourself: Becoming the Love You Needed

If the root of brokenness is often *childhood trauma,* then the cure begins with **re-parenting yourself.** This is the sacred practice of learning to relate to yourself the way a loving parent would – firmly, gently, and with enduring grace. It's how you replace the internalized voices of criticism, neglect, or conditional love with compassion, patience, and truth.

When you fear rejection or abandonment, your inner child is often the one feeling it. That little version of you wants to know: *"Am I still loved, even if I'm scared?"* In re-parenting yourself, you would assert, *"You are loved by me always, no matter what they do or say."*

Re-parenting isn't regression; it's redemption. Re-parenting redirects the way we speak to, think of, and treat ourselves. It means speaking to the hurting parts of you that never received affirmation and telling them the truth they've always needed to hear. It means thinking of yourself as someone who was born with intrinsic value because you were created in God's image. It also means treating yourself as a loving caregiver would with unconditional love and consistent care.

Try beginning here:

- **Notice the voice inside.**
  When self-criticism arises, ask whose voice it sounds like: your own or someone from your past? Does this sound like my *mother, father, grandparent,* ex, etc.? Naming it creates distance and power.

- **Offer warmth and patience.**
  Say to yourself:
  "I'm allowed to make mistakes."
  "I'm learning to be kind to myself."

These simple statements begin to rewire the emotional nervous system.

- **Practice daily care.**
  Feed yourself well. Rest. Set boundaries. Keep promises to yourself. Small acts of nurture signal safety to your inner child.

- **Challenge the "deserve" narrative.**
  Replace *"Do I deserve this?"* with *"Can I allow this?"*

Worthiness isn't earned; it's remembered.
"Deserve" asks if something has earned access to you.
"Allow" asks if something aligns with you.

Re-parenting transforms self-abandonment into self-advocacy. You stop waiting for others to give what you can now give to yourself: consistency, compassion, and care. This is where whole healing begins, not when someone finally chooses you, but when you finally choose yourself.

For a complete reference chart of ARC language, see **Appendix C**.

> *"Until you learn to nurture yourself, every relationship becomes a search for your missing parent."*

If the idea of becoming the love you needed brings emotion to the surface, pause here. In your journal, write a letter to the younger version of yourself who learned to survive without consistent care.

Filling Your Own Cup

When I knew I could no longer continue in my long-term relationship, it wasn't because of a single argument or betrayal. It was the moment I realized my cup was empty, feeling unseen, unheard and unloved. I had been in a one-sided relationship, one that I had to sustain with all of my emotional effort while he simply received.

One day before this point, I had gleefully asked him if he knew my love language. He paused before answering, "Quality time." My heart sank. I knew exactly what his was – *words of affirmation* – and he proudly confirmed it. In that moment, I realized he wasn't truly invested in knowing me. He knew my favorite color because I had mentioned it when he wore a shirt that color, but beyond that, he had never been curious about what filled me.

What I longed for wasn't complicated. As a serial entrepreneur, my love language *acts of service* was about partnership, about someone who showed up with encouragement, advice, or even just presence. Yet when I told him that, he seemed surprised. That surprise told me everything: he hadn't really been listening or paying attention to me.

Dr. Gary Chapman, author of *The Five Love Languages*, teaches that we all experience love differently and must learn to "fill our partner's love tank" in the way that they best receive it (Chapman 1992) I had read his book years earlier and found it fascinating. I always imagined love like a cup being filled, something that needs consistent care and attention. Meanwhile, I was in a relationship where my cup stayed empty.

I wanted to fight for what we had, but I realized I had nothing to fight *with* or *for.* Those two prepositions – "with" and "for" – defined my brokenness at the time. My cup was empty, so I had nothing to fight *with*. Moreover, when I could no longer see what we were even fighting *for*, I knew it was over.

I had spent so long accusing him of not pouring into me through my love language of acts of service or even my secondary one, gifts, that I hadn't realized how long I'd gone without pouring into myself. The truth was I was depleted because I had outsourced my wholeness.

When I finally accepted that, I made a choice: to stop waiting for him to fill my cup and start refilling it myself. I began to respect, affirm, and nurture my own needs again. I recommitted to my wholeness.

No relationship can survive when there is nothing to fight *with* or *for.* However, wholeness begins when you decide you are worth fighting *for*.

Before you can love anyone else in a whole and healthy way, you must first learn how to meet your own needs. Keep in mind, you are not the source of love, but you are responsible for how you receive it, respond to it, and live from it. Wholeness begins when you stop waiting for someone else to do what you're unwilling to do for yourself. For instance, if someone disrespected you, the healing is not found in demanding respect from others; it's found in learning to respect yourself. If someone betrayed you, the healing comes from rebuilding your trust in *you*. If someone denied your truth, your healing is to affirm it daily until your soul believes it again.

When you start doing for yourself what you once expected from others, you reclaim your power. You stop outsourcing your wholeness. You no longer live from the scarcity of "what they didn't do" but from the abundance of "what I can now give myself."

The Wholeness Exchange

What They Did	What You Must Do for Yourself
Disrespect	Self-Respect
Disloyalty	Trust Yourself
Denial	Affirm Your Truth
Dismissive	Be Attentive to Your Needs
Harsh	Be Gentle and Kind
Cruel	Show Yourself Compassion
Cheap/Stingy	Be Generous With Your Love and Care

This exchange is not about mirroring their actions; it's about rewriting your own emotional code. Each act of self-nourishment becomes a quiet revolution against every moment you abandoned yourself to be loved by someone else.

When you fill your own needs first:

- You no longer confuse attention with affection
- You can receive love without fear of losing it
- You become emotionally self-sufficient, able to *share* love rather than *seek* it

This is the foundation of *whole relationships*: giving and receiving love from a place of fullness, not emptiness. Remember, wholeness is not built by finding someone who won't break you; it's built by becoming someone who can't be broken.

> *"Connection helps you understand yourself; commitment teaches you to trust yourself."*

Before beginning Part III, consider completing the ARC of Self pages in the workbook. Integration happens when insight meets practice, and there is no benefit to skipping that step.

Confidence stabilizes identity. Commitment sustains it. Yet stability alone does not guarantee clarity. You may be loyal to yourself and still feel uncertain about what you actually need to flourish. Wholeness requires not only self-trust, but self-understanding.

In the next section, we turn to the deeper question: What does your soul require? Because commitment without clarity can become rigidity, but commitment guided by insight becomes wisdom.

PART II REVIEW: THE JOURNEY WITHIN

Wholeness begins within. The journey within is ultimately a journey toward truth: truth about your patterns, your needs, your values, and your becoming. Awareness opens our eyes to who we are. Respect teaches us to honor that truth. Confidence empowers us to live it out.

Part II walked you through the understanding the architecture of your inner world, your **A.R.C. of Self**:

- **Self-A**wareness
- **Self-R**espect
- **Self-C**onfidence

The ARC of Self shows you *how* wholeness is lived, practiced, and sustained. It becomes the internal compass that guides your relationships, your decisions, and your patterns of connection. Once whole, it stabilizes your identity, restores your voice, and reclaims your worth.

Each chapter invited you to:

- face your truth without shame,
- honor your needs without guilt,
- and act from alignment rather than fear.

Before you can pour into someone else, you must learn how to pour into yourself. This means committing to your wholeness first.

You've explored the foundation of healthy boundaries, emotional honesty, and the self-governance required for whole love. Your becoming is not about perfection, but about presence, showing up for yourself with truth, courage, and compassion. Internal alignment prepares you for relational clarity. Now we turn to the needs that shape how that alignment is expressed.

Before beginning Part III, review the affirmations that support connection and commitment to self in **Appendix E** *along with the related prompts in* **Appendix F**. *You should also express your thoughts and feelings in your journal.*

PART III

THE SOUL ESSENTIALS

Understanding the Needs that Shape Us

8

SOUL NEEDS

Awareness opens our eyes to who we are. Respect teaches us to honor that truth. Confidence empowers us to live it out. Together, **awareness, respect, and confidence** form the ARC of Self, the foundation for every whole relationship. Through them, we learn to connect inwardly before we can connect outwardly. Then we must commit to honoring, nurturing and expressing this truth.

When you commit to yourself, you strengthen trust in your own voice and choices. You begin to move from self-awareness to *soul awareness* – from recognizing your patterns to understanding the needs beneath them. Self-awareness tells you what you do. Soul awareness reveals why it matters. It is the practice of honoring your God-given design with clarity and compassion. Essentially, self-awareness is the soul's mirror.

Commitment sustains that identity over time. Yet stability alone does not guarantee clarity. You may be loyal to yourself and still feel uncertain about what you actually need to flourish. To live wholly, you must understand the architecture beneath your behavior, the needs that shape your boundaries, desires, and convictions. This is the language of the soul.

So, now we'll explore the deeper blueprint beneath our behaviors, the sacred needs that drive, shape, and sustain us. Because once you understand your *soul needs*, you can stop chasing external validation and start living in alignment with who you were designed to be.

Understanding Soul Needs

Everyone has needs. Some are about survival (food, sleep, air, water). Others are about flourishing (belonging, meaning, purpose). In this book we distinguish between **universal** and **unique** soul needs so you can name what is non-negotiable in your life and relationships and stop confusing preferences with requirements.

Unnamed needs turn into silent expectations. Silent expectations turn into resentment. Naming your needs is not selfish; it is how you protect your peace, direct your choices, and invite alignment with others.

Universal vs. Unique Soul Needs

Every human life includes layered needs that emerge from our being:

- **Physiological:** food, sleep, air, water
- **Physical:** clothing, touch, shelter, movement
- **Emotional:** love, security, attention
- **Psychological:** autonomy, acceptance, relatedness
- **Soul:** truth, love, faith, connection, peace

Your **soul needs** are the integrators. They align how you live (doing) with who you are (being). They include two components:

- **Universal Soul Needs** are shared by all people. They are rooted in truth and necessary for well-being and healthy connection.
- **Unique Soul Needs** reflect how your **purpose**, **personality**, and **perspective** shape **(PPP)** dictate what *you* require to thrive and how they're resourced by your **talent, traits**, and **time (TTT).**

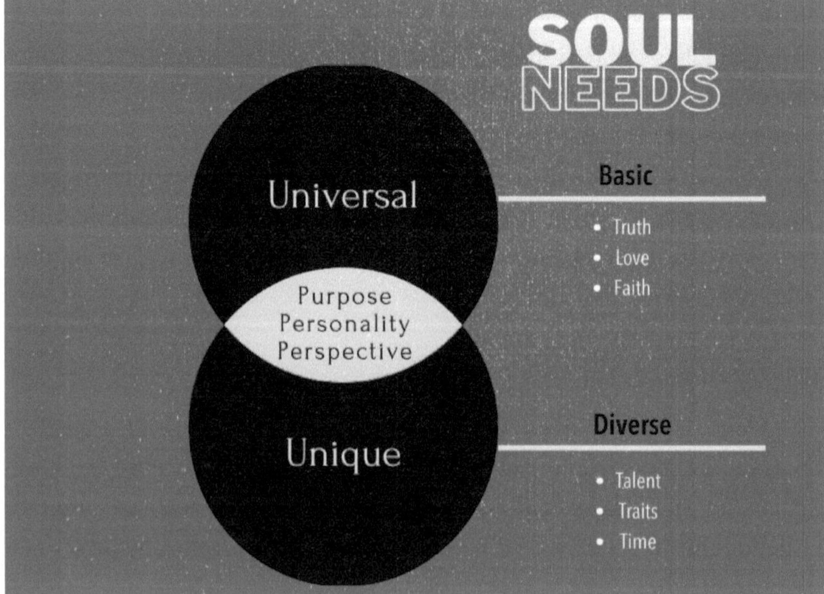

Soul needs are not demands, flaws or weaknesses. They are signals shaped by who you are. To avoid over-analysis, consider using the Soul Needs pages in the workbook. They are designed to help you name what matters most without turning insight into pressure.

Universal Soul Needs (The Core Three)

- **Truth** – Living in reality; honesty with self and others; congruence between values and behavior.
- **Faith** – Trusting what you cannot control; hope and meaning that steady you during uncertainty.
- **Love** – Being seen, valued, and cared for; giving and receiving care in ways that honor dignity.

These three are the *soil* of wholeness: **truth** grounds you, **faith** steadies you, and **love** nourishes you.

Unique Soul Needs (How Your Design Shows Up)

Your unique needs arise where who you are **(PPP)** meets what you use to live it **(TTT).**

PPP — Shape

- **Purpose** – What your life is *for.*
    - o *Examples:* self-expression and innovation (creativity-centered purpose); compassion and altruism (service-centered purpose).
- **Personality** – The patterns of how you engage.
    - o *Examples:* solitude and reflection (introversion); frequent interaction and stimulation (extraversion).
- **Perspective** – Your beliefs, values, and worldview.
    - o *Examples:* communion with God/inner peace (spiritual lens); knowledge and understanding (scientific lens).

TTT — Resources

- **Talent** – Your God-given abilities and developed skills. Your needs include *spaces and rhythms to use them.*
    - *Example:* A gifted songwriter may need uninterrupted creative blocks weekly.
- **Traits** – Stable dispositions/temperament that govern energy and tolerance. Your needs include *environments that fit your wiring.*
    - *Example:* A high emotional sensitivity trait may need low-conflict processing and clear tone.
- **Time** – The cadence and margins that keep you whole. Your needs include *repetitions, durations, and recovery windows.*
    - *Example:* You may need 24 hours of notice for plan changes or a daily 60-minute quiet hour.

UNIQUE NEEDS = *PPP (shape) expressed through TTT (resources) in service of TLF (universal needs)*

Needs vs. Wants vs. Strategies

- A **need** is a non-negotiable condition for your well-being (e.g., emotional safety).
- A **want** is a preference (e.g., Friday date nights).
- A **strategy** is one way to meet a need (e.g., "text me every morning" to meet the need for connection).

Hold strategies loosely, but hold needs firmly.

> *"Unmet needs do not disappear. They distort behavior."*

Putting It Together: Examples

A worship leader (purpose) who is introverted (personality) with a contemplative viewpoint (perspective) using **talent** (music), **traits** (high sensitivity), **time** (focused time blocks) may need:

- 2–3 protected creative mornings/week + quiet debrief after conflict to keep Truth/Love/Faith alive while serving others

An activist community organizer who is highly extroverted using **talent** (mobilizing), **traits** (high energy), **time** (fast cycles) may need:

- Frequent collaborative wins + clear weekly goals to sustain hope/meaning **(Faith)** and belonging **(Love)** anchored in demonstrated need **(Truth)**

Here are examples associated with necessary time:

- Talent (songwriting) + Traits (high sensitivity) + Time (mornings): "I need two *uninterrupted creative mornings* weekly to write and reset."

- Talent (strategy) + Traits (introversion) + Time (early afternoons): "I need a daily *focus hour* after lunch to think without meetings."

The Zero-Tolerance Policy

Your Soul Needs are **foundational** because they arise from your authentic self and the natural state of your peace. Non-negotiable doesn't mean rigid or unkind; it means **consistent.** People closest to you should **recognize, respect,** and **participate** in meeting these needs, and you should do the same for theirs.

Seeing your need is step one. Saying your need is step two. Next, we'll convert soul mirror insights into clear requests and compassionate boundaries that protect peace without punishing people. Compassionate enforcement looks like:

- **Name it:** "Truth is a core need for me. I need honest updates, even when the news is hard."
- **Request it:** "When plans change, please tell me directly the same day."
- **Protect it:** "If we can't maintain honesty, I will step back to preserve my peace."

Here is another example:

- **Name it:** "I do my best work in quiet hours. It keeps me grounded in truth and peace."
- **Request it:** "Could we keep 9–11 a.m. as no-meeting time on Tuesdays/Thursdays?"
- **Protect it:** "I'll be in a focus session then; I'll respond right after."

Red Flags When Needs Are Unmet

- You chronically **explain away** misalignment.
- You feel **anxious, resentful or numb** in key relationships.
- You over-invest in **strategies** (checking phones, ultimatums) instead of addressing the **need** (safety, truth, respect).

If grief or anger arises as you recognize unmet soul needs, pause here. Let your journal hold what was missed, ignored, or postponed.

Honor the universal. **Articulate** the unique. **Resource** them wisely. When you live by truth, sustained by faith, and expressed through love, communicating how *you* uniquely need those to be met, you stop outsourcing your wholeness and start living it.

Before moving forward, pause and consider which of your universal needs (truth, love, or faith) feels most neglected. Notice how your unique design (purpose, personality, and perspective) shapes what those needs require in daily life. Clarity is the beginning of alignment.

While seeing your soul needs is the beginning, serving them wisely is the work. In the next chapter, we will explore the stages of maturity that move a need from awareness to faithful expression.

---

*To explore your universal and unique soul needs more deeply, complete the "Soul Needs Discovery Worksheet" (**Appendix D**).*

9

THE FOUR STAGES OF SERVING SOUL NEEDS

Every human being has soul needs – deep, inner requirements that make us feel valued, seen, safe, supported, respected, and loved. These needs are personal and often unspoken, yet they shape our relationships more than we realize.

To honor someone's soul needs is an act of humility and love: true **servanthood**. However, we cannot serve another's soul if we do not first recognize, respect, and honor our own. Self-awareness is the foundation of relational servanthood.

When soul needs are neglected – whether our own or our partner's – relationships begin to break down. A person whose needs are chronically unmet may disconnect emotionally, seek fulfillment elsewhere or remain physically present while silently withholding love, respect, intimacy or effort. Another person may recognize their partner's needs but refuse to meet them because *their own needs have been ignored*. This creates an emotional stalemate: two people are together, yet both dissatisfied, unfulfilled, and quietly retreating.

No relationship can thrive in that state. This is why it is essential to understand this truth: **A whole relationship isn't perfect; it's practiced.** It is the daily exchange of two imperfect, self-aware, surrendered souls serving one another with intention and emotional maturity. Wholeness emerges when both people commit to meeting soul needs consistently, not occasionally.

Serving the soul is a process that moves through four deliberate stages:

1. **Acknowledgement** – Do I know my soul needs?
2. **Analysis** – Are my soul needs being met?
3. **Actualization** – What happens when my soul needs are or are not met?
4. **Attainment** – How do I get my soul needs met in a healthy, whole way?

These four stages form the roadmap for emotional maturity and relational wholeness. Each stage builds on the last, guiding us from internal discovery to external alignment.

When we learn to move through these stages not once, but continuously, we develop the wisdom to recognize our soul's voice, the clarity to communicate our needs, and the maturity to serve the soul of another without losing ourselves.

Now, let's begin with the first stage: **Acknowledgement**

Acknowledgement

The truth is that we are *always* aware of our soul needs but just not always consciously. Even when we cannot articulate what we require emotionally, spiritually, or relationally, our behavior reveals the truth on our behalf. This is why we react strongly when someone ignores us, dismisses us, or fails to treat us in a way that aligns with our deepest wiring.

Our soul speaks in signals, including complaints, sensitivities, irritations, frustrations, or withdrawals. These are not "overreactions." They are indicators.

Your soul is essentially crying out:

"See me. Hear me. Honor what I need."

Acknowledgement comes in two forms:

1. Subconscious Acknowledgement

This level of acknowledgement shows up through:

- Complaints
- Repeated conflicts
- Resentment or shutdown
- Jealousy or insecurity
- Avoidance or co-dependency
- Feeling unseen or dismissed

At this stage, the person may not know *why* they react the way they do. They only know something feels off. Their soul is signaling unmet needs long before their mind can interpret them.

This is where most relationships struggle. People feel the pain of an unmet need but cannot name it, explain it, or guide their partner to support it. As a result, partners respond to *symptoms* instead of to the *root cause*.

Subconscious acknowledgement creates noise, not clarity.

2. Conscious Acknowledgement

Conscious acknowledgement is when we intentionally identify, name, and honor what our soul requires to thrive.

A consciously aware person can say:

- "I need reassurance."
- "I need respect in how you speak to me."
- "I need partnership, not performance."
- "I need emotional safety before I can be vulnerable."
- "I need to feel understood, not managed."

This level of self-knowledge allows you to:

- set boundaries,
- communicate clearly,
- choose compatible partners,
- avoid self-abandonment, and
- invite someone into the truth of who you are.

However, acknowledgement reveals character, too, because if you are aware and **broken**, you may:

- communicate your need but tolerate its neglect,
- accept behaviors that violate your soul,
- hope someone will change rather than require it,
- shrink yourself to keep the peace,
- demand nothing and resent everything.

Acknowledgement without wholeness leads to self-betrayal. However, if you are aware and **whole**, you will:

- articulate your needs with clarity,
- honor them as non-negotiable truths,
- require reciprocity,
- respect your partner's needs as well,
- choose alignment over attachment.

Acknowledgement becomes empowerment.

Why Acknowledgement Matters

No one can serve your soul without direction. No one can meet a need you have not named. No one can honor what you continually ignore.

Acknowledgement is the first step toward emotional maturity because it moves the conversation from:

"You keep hurting me…"

to

"This is what my soul needs to feel loved, safe, and whole."

Once acknowledgement is gained, the next stage becomes possible:

Analysis, where we examine whether our soul needs are truly being met and what happens when they are not.

Analysis

Acknowledgement tells you *what* your soul needs, and analysis tells you *whether* those needs are being met.

This stage requires honesty, reflection, and emotional courage. Many people stop at acknowledgement because analysis forces a deeper confrontation:

> "Is the life I'm living actually nurturing my soul or am I surviving on emotional crumbs?"

Wholeness requires evaluation. Love cannot be sustained where needs are ignored.

What Analysis Really Means

Analysis is not judgment, blame, or criticism. It is the ability to step back and ask the hard but necessary questions:

- *Is this relationship meeting my core soul needs?*
- *Am I consistently nourished emotionally, mentally, spiritually, and socially?*
- *Do I feel seen, valued, safe, and supported?*
- *Does this person respond to my needs or dismiss them?*
- *Am I meeting their soul needs?*

Analysis looks at the health, not the hope. Broken people analyze through **fear**:

- "If I speak up, they might leave."
- "Maybe I'm asking for too much."
- "If I stop giving, they might stop loving me."

Whole people analyze through **truth**:

- "This pattern is harming my soul."
- "We cannot grow unless we acknowledge what's missing."
- "Both of our needs matter, not just one."

One is driven by fear of loss, and the other is driven by desire for alignment.

The Three Layers of Analysis

A mature analysis looks at the relationship from three different vantage points:

1. Internal Analysis (Self → Self)

Ask yourself:

- Do I feel fulfilled or drained?
- Are my boundaries respected?
- Do I feel emotionally safe?
- Am I abandoning myself to keep the peace?

This is where you measure your own wellbeing.

2. Relational Analysis (Self → Other)

Ask:

- Does this person *consistently* show up for my soul?
- Do they respond with care when I communicate my needs?
- Is their love expressed or merely implied?
- Do their actions align with their words?

This reveals the truth about the relationship dynamic.

3. Reciprocal Analysis (Self ↔ Other)

Ask:

- Are we serving each other's soul needs?
- Is this relationship balanced?
- Am I the only one giving, fixing, or sacrificing?
- Do we practice mutual care?

This shows whether the relationship is whole or lopsided.

Analysis Without Action Is Self-Deception

Some people analyze endlessly but refuse to make changes. This is emotional procrastination. They know the truth, but:

- fear the consequences,
- minimize their own needs, or
- hope time will fix what honesty should.

However, clarity is useless without courage. Analysis becomes emotional maturity when you are willing to:

- acknowledge what is happening,
- address the imbalance,
- make adjustments,
- communicate openly,
- set boundaries, and
- respond to the truth rather than avoid it.

Why Analysis Matters

You cannot reach actualization, the next stage, until you understand:

1. **Whether your needs are met**
2. **How unmet needs affect you**
3. **What patterns are emerging in the relationship**

Analysis gives you the data your soul needs to thrive. It turns emotional noise into emotional knowledge. Once you know what is happening, you can begin to understand why, and that moves you naturally into the next stage:

Actualization — What happens when your soul needs are or are not being met?

Actualization

Acknowledgement identifies your soul needs. Analysis evaluates whether those needs are being met. Actualization reveals ***how*** **those needs, met or unmet, show up in your life**.

Actualization is the stage where internal truth becomes external behavior. It is the point where what you feel becomes what you *do*.

Whether your soul needs are fulfilled or neglected, the effects will manifest through:

- your emotions,
- your attitudes,
- your reactions,
- your communication,
- your level of peace, and
- your ability to connect with others.

Actualization exposes what the soul already knows.

Actualization When Needs Are NOT Met

Unmet soul needs create emotional erosion. They chip away at confidence, clarity, and connection until the relationship becomes a cycle of survival. When needs are unmet, we see actualization in patterns such as:

1. Emotional Withdrawal

You pull away to protect yourself.

- Less communication
- Less excitement
- Less vulnerability
- Less presence

This happens not because you don't care, but because your soul is trying to conserve energy.

2. Irritability & Sensitivity

Small things trigger big reactions.

- Tone feels like disrespect
- Delays feel like rejection
- Mistakes feel like betrayal

Your soul is on high alert.

3. Performance or Pretending

You hide your real feelings:

- Smiling while hurting
- Agreeing while resenting
- Saying "it's fine" when it's not

Pretending is emotional exhaustion in disguise.

4. Resentment

Bitterness emerges when your soul recognizes imbalance:

- "I give more than I receive."
- "I'm always the one sacrificing."
- "They don't value what I need."

Resentment is unspoken pain hardened over time.

5. Self-Abandonment

You minimize your needs:

- "It's not that big of a deal."
- "I don't want to start a fight."
- "They have more on their plate than I do."

> *"Self-abandonment is the soul's quiet death."*

6. Disconnection or Distaste

When needs are chronically unmet, affection decreases:

- You feel less drawn to them
- You stop initiating or responding
- You feel distant even in their presence
- You develop disdain

The connection fades because the nourishment stopped.

7. Fight, Flight, Freeze, or Fawn

Unmet needs activate survival patterns:

- **Fight:** arguing, defensiveness
- **Flight:** avoidance, isolation, withdrawal
- **Freeze:** shutting down emotionally
- **Fawn:** over-accommodating to keep peace

These are not personality traits; they are protection mechanisms.

Actualization When Needs ARE Met

When soul needs are honored, the relationship becomes a safe, fertile ground where connection can grow. When needs are met, we see actualization in patterns like:

1. Emotional Security

You feel safe bringing your whole self.

- You share openly
- You let your guard down
- You express truthfully
- You trust deeply

Your soul relaxes.

2. Consistent Peace

You no longer brace for disappointment.

- No tension
- No fear
- No walking on eggshells

You exist in calm, not chaos.

3. Increased Intimacy

When needs are fulfilled:

- affection grows,
- communication strengthens,
- connection deepens, and
- love becomes the natural language.

Intimacy is easier when you're emotionally fed.

4. Gratitude & Reciprocity

Being cared for inspires you to give back.

- You show appreciation
- You initiate affection
- You serve your partner joyfully
- You meet their needs willingly

Reciprocity becomes effortless.

5. Respect & Admiration

Meeting soul needs builds trust and honor.

- You look at your partner with pride
- You value how they show up
- You admire how they love you

Respect becomes the root; love becomes the fruit.

6. Alignment & Harmony

When soul needs are met:

- conflict decreases,
- clarity increases,
- connection stabilizes.

You feel like you're moving "with" each other, not against each other.

Why Actualization Matters

Actualization is the evidence. It reveals:

- the true condition of your connection
- the impact of unmet needs
- the potential when needs are fulfilled

You cannot ignore actualization. It is the soul speaking through behavior. It is the heart's report card. Once you understand how your soul responds to what it receives or lacks, you are finally ready for the next stage:

Attainment — How do you get your soul needs met?

Attainment

Acknowledgement tells you what you need. Analysis tells you whether you're getting it. Actualization shows how unmet or fulfilled needs affect you. Attainment is the stage where you learn how to get your soul needs met in a *healthy, sustainable, reciprocal* way.

Attainment is not manipulation or control. It is the mature stewardship of your soul through honest communication, wise selection, and consistent boundaries. More specifically, it is the stage where you take responsibility for:

- communicating clearly,
- choosing wisely,
- honoring your boundaries,
- responding to unmet needs, and
- aligning with people capable of serving your soul.

Attainment is the practice of getting your needs met through wholeness, not woundedness.

What Attainment Really Means

Attainment is not about "getting what you want." It is about receiving what your soul requires to operate at its highest emotional, spiritual, and relational capacity. It happens through:

1. **Communication**
2. **Compatibility**
3. **Capacity**
4. **Consistency**

Every healthy relationship rests on these four pillars. Let's break them down.

1. Communication: Expressing Your Soul Needs Clearly

You cannot attain what you will not articulate. Whole communication sounds like:

- "This is what I need to feel connected."
- "I feel loved when you… "
- "I need clarity, reassurance, or gentleness in moments like this."
- "It matters to me that you honor this boundary."

Broken communication sounds like:

- hints
- complaints
- silence
- sarcasm
- hoping they "just know"

Communication is your first tool of attainment because it invites your partner into the truth of your soul. Wholeness communicates. Brokenness compensates.

2. Compatibility: Choosing People Who Can Serve Your Soul

Some people care about you but cannot meet your soul needs. This is not because they are bad, but because you are *incompatible*.

Compatibility means:

- your needs match their natural expressions
- their strengths align with what your soul requires
- their weaknesses do not consistently injure you
- your emotional languages are complementary
- their capacity matches your connection style

Compatibility determines whether your soul can thrive in that relationship. You cannot attain what the other person does not have to give.

3. Capacity: Ensuring They Have the Emotional Tools

Capacity and compatibility are not the same.

- Compatibility asks:
  "Is this person naturally aligned with what I need?"
- Capacity asks:
  "Is this person emotionally equipped to meet my needs consistently?"

A person may have:

- Good intentions but poor tools
- Love but no emotional vocabulary
- Desire but no self-awareness
- Passion but no discipline
- Connection but no consistency

Capacity is the emotional infrastructure that supports your soul. If they cannot self-regulate, communicate or empathize, they will struggle to serve your needs even if they want to. Attainment requires honesty about someone's actual ability, not their potential.

4. Consistency: Receiving Your Needs in a Sustainable Way

Attainment is not about momentary effort. Consistency is:

- predictable care
- repeated follow-through
- emotional reliability
- effort without prompting
- a steady pattern of showing up

Consistency builds trust while inconsistency builds trauma. A soul cannot thrive on occasional affection and sporadic effort. It needs predictable nourishment. Attainment asks: "Is this person steady in how they love me?"

Healthy Attainment vs. Unhealthy Attainment

Healthy attainment flows from wholeness:

- honest communication
- wise boundaries
- aligned partnerships
- choosing emotionally healthy people
- honoring your own needs
- walking away when necessary

Unhealthy attainment flows from brokenness:

- manipulation and control
- fear-based clinging
- self-abandonment
- guilt-based love
- proving your worth
- accepting the bare minimum

Attainment is only successful when your approach honors both:

- Your soul
- The other person's freedom

Anything else is coercion, not connection.

Attainment Is About Requiring, Not Just Receiving

You cannot attain what you do not require. You cannot require what you do not respect. You cannot respect what you do not believe you deserve.

Attainment demands:

- self-worth
- emotional maturity
- courage
- boundaries
- clarity
- willingness to walk away

Attainment is not passive. It is the active stewardship of your soul.

Why Attainment Matters

Attainment is the stage where:

- you stop settling,
- you stop shrinking,
- you stop hoping,
- you stop begging,
- you stop excusing, and
- you start aligning.

Attainment is the moment your soul says:
"I will no longer survive in places where I'm meant to thrive."

It is the spiritual and emotional commitment to position yourself in relationships where your soul is honored consistently, not occasionally.

Once you learn how to get your needs met, you become capable of the final piece of emotional maturity: **Soul Discernment**, the master skill developed by moving through all four stages. It's the natural outcome of mastering the four stages:

1. **Acknowledgement** — "I know it."
2. **Analysis** — "I examine it."
3. **Actualization** — "I feel the effects of it."
4. **Attainment** — "I pursue what aligns with it."

Discernment — "I choose wisely, consistently, and maturely."

You do not need to move through these stages all at once. In fact, trying to do so often leads to confusion or self-criticism. The companion workbook offers a brief stage-identification reflection to help you identify in which stage you currently are. Let that be enough for now.

The Maturity That Emerges from the Four Stages

Emotional immaturity comes from a lack of internal clarity, but emotional maturity comes from a deep internal understanding. True emotional maturity begins with **soul discernment**, understanding *what* your soul needs, *why* it needs it, and *how* those needs shape your behavior, relationships, and patterns. Discernment is the wisdom that emerges when clarity meets courage.

When you recognize your soul needs, something powerful happens: You stop reacting blindly and start responding intentionally. You stop blaming others for what you never named. You stop expecting people to meet needs you have never communicated. You stop abandoning yourself to preserve relationships that were never designed to carry the weight of your soul.

Emotional maturity is not simply the ability to stay calm under pressure or respond gently when triggered. Soul discernment is what transforms emotional reactivity into emotional responsibility. It produces the following outcomes:

1. Brings Clarity

People who lack emotional clarity operate from:

- knee-jerk reactions
- childhood wounds
- insecurity
- fear-based assumptions

Meanwhile, people who have discernment operate from:

- truth
- self-understanding
- groundedness
- internal alignment

Clarity reduces confusion, conflict and chaos. You cannot be emotionally mature while emotionally confused.

2. Prevents Projection

When you know your own needs, triggers, and wounds, you stop projecting them onto others. Instead of:

- assuming your partner is ignoring you,
- assuming someone's tone means disrespect,
- assuming distance equals disinterest,
- …you can pause and ask:
  "Is this my fear speaking or my soul?"

Emotional maturity grows when you take responsibility for your inner world instead of forcing someone else to carry it.

3. Strengthens Communication

When you know your soul needs, you communicate clearly rather than chaotically. Your words become:

- specific,
- grounded,
- honest,
- direct.

You can say:

- "I need reassurance,"
  not
- "You never care about me."

You can say:

- "I feel disconnected,"
  not
- "You always pull away."

Discernment creates language that leads to connection rather than conflict.

4. Builds Healthy Boundaries

When you know your needs, you know your limits. You stop over-giving. You stop overcompensating. You stop pleasing, performing, and pretending.

Healthy boundaries are not walls. They're instructions. Boundaries tell the world:

"This is how you love me without injuring me."

Emotional maturity is impossible without boundaries rooted in self-respect.

5. Increases Acknowledgement

Once you understand your needs, you recognize:

- who is aligned with you,
- who is capable of loving you,
- who can serve your soul, and
- who cannot.

Soul discernment grows because you are no longer choosing relationships based on:

- chemistry
- loneliness
- trauma bonding
- fantasy

You choose based on **alignment**, which is the highest form of emotional wisdom.

6. Promotes Reciprocity

You can only give what you understand. You can only serve what you can see. You can only honor in others what you have honored in yourself.

When you know your soul needs, you become more sensitive and responsive to the needs of others. You recognize that love is not a performance but a partnership.

This shifts your relationships from:

transaction → transformation

and

demand → service

Emotional maturity is the ability to give love in a way that honors both souls.

7. Soul Discernment Creates Accountability

When you understand your triggers, patterns, and needs, you stop blaming others for your behavior. You can admit:

- "I shut down because I felt overwhelmed."
- "I reacted out of fear, not truth."
- "I'm responsible for managing my emotions."

This is emotional adulthood. Accountability deepens intimacy, and blame destroys it.

8. Produces Emotional Stability

Emotional maturity is not the absence of emotion. It is the stability within it. When your soul is understood and nourished:

- you regulate better
- you react less
- you recover faster
- you speak wiser
- you love safer

> *"Emotional maturity begins with soul discernment."*

Soul discernment is not about finding perfect people. It is about refusing to participate in patterns that starve your soul. When you understand what nourishes you, you stop romanticizing what depletes you. Your emotions no longer control you; you understand them. Your triggers no longer surprise you; you anticipate them. Your wounds no longer define you; you heal them.

Discernment is not merely emotional intelligence; it is spiritual maturity expressed relationally. It reflects the wisdom to see clearly, the humility to examine honestly, and the courage to act faithfully. This is the kind of grounded, whole love Christ modeled, not reactive, not self-erasing, but attuned, honest, and deeply aware of what nourishes the soul.

Serving the Soul, the Highest Expression of Love

A whole relationship is impossible without soul discernment because meeting soul needs is intentional, not accidental. Soul discernment teaches you:

- what you require,
- how to communicate it,
- how to attain it,
- how to honor someone else's needs,
- and how to build emotional maturity through understanding and alignment.

This chapter forms the foundation for serving the soul in relationships, both yours and theirs. When we understand our soul needs and learn how to honor them with maturity, something sacred happens: we gain the ability to honor another person's soul with wisdom, compassion, and clarity. This is the essence of **servanthood** in Whole Relationships, not servitude, not self-erasure, but the intentional act of nurturing another person's humanity with integrity and discernment.

Servanthood is not about what you give, but *how* you give. It is not about doing more; it is about loving wisely. It is not about meeting demands, but meeting needs. It is not about losing yourself, but showing up as your whole self so you can love from overflow, not depletion.

When you practice the four stages (Acknowledgement, Analysis, Actualization, and Attainment) you develop soul discernment, which is what allows you to love someone in a way that is sustainable, balanced, reciprocal, and spiritually aligned. It helps you see what is being asked of you, what belongs to you, and what does not. It teaches you to give without overgiving, care without controlling, and serve without shrinking. Again, this is the mature love Christ modeled: **honest, humble, discerning,** and **deeply attuned to the soul**.

Whole love is not built on emotion alone. It is built on the willingness to:

- serve each other well
- recognize needs before they become wounds
- respond with empathy instead of ego
- offer care that strengthens rather than depletes
- create a relationship where both souls can thrive, not just survive

Soul discernment prepares the heart for this kind of love. Servanthood makes it possible. Together, they form the bridge to our next chapter: learning to love with **Soul Intelligence**, the spiritual and emotional wisdom that allows two people to walk in wholeness, humility, and purpose.

10

LOVING WITH SOUL INTELLIGENCE

Soul intelligence is what discernment looks like in action. Discernment gives you clarity about your soul and the soul of another. Soul intelligence gives you the wisdom to *respond* to that clarity with love, empathy, humility, and alignment. It is the ability to perceive the deeper emotional truth beneath someone's behavior and serve their soul without abandoning your own. It is the capacity to read what your soul is signaling (truth, love, and faith) in real time and to respond in alignment through clear requests, compassionate boundaries, and consistent actions that honor your purpose, personality, and perspective. In other words, it is a practiced skill of *noticing* your inner signals (TLF), *naming* the real need (PPP), and *meeting* it wisely using your unique resources (TTT) so your *doing* stays congruent with your *being*. This keeps you whole.

Here is a quick breakdown of:

- **What it reads:** Truth • Love • Faith (universal needs)
- **How it applies:** PPP × TTT (your shape and resources)
- **What it produces:** Clear requests, compassionate boundaries, reliable follow-through

You can remember this easily as: **Notice. Name. Nourish.**

- Notice what your soul is signaling – truth, love, faith
- Name the need beneath the feeling – your purpose, personality, perspective
- Nourish the need using your unique resources – your talents, traits, time

Soul Mirror

Many of us live like a cracked mirror. The mirror still reflects an image, but the reflection is distorted. Instead of repairing the mirror, we try to polish the surface — working harder, achieving more, pleasing people, hiding our pain — hoping the reflection will somehow look better.

The "Soul Mirror" is your moment-to-moment awareness of what your soul is signaling and how clearly your relationships reflect it back to you. A clear mirror allows you to recognize needs accurately and honor them wisely. When you feel reactive, ask:

(?) What is my soul signaling right now, and is this relationship reflecting it clearly or distorting it?

Recognizing Needs

A clear soul mirror does not reflect only your own needs; it helps you perceive the needs of others accurately. Recognizing the feelings and needs of others is the first step towards empathy and a healthy connection (Rumie.org n.d.). We can detect emotional signals by paying attention to other people's body language, including their posture, tone of voice, facial expressions, and other nonverbal cues. Nonverbal cues can communicate a lot about a person's thoughts and feelings. Often, these cues reveal what words conceal. However, recognition is not maturity in itself. It is awareness without yet requiring action.

Respecting Needs

Recognition sees the need. Respect honors the need. While recognition acknowledges the presence of another person's need, respect treats that need as worthy of consideration, dignity, and care. This is why "recognition" and "respect" are distinct concepts.

In a whole relationship, both partners must do more than notice each other's emotional signals. They must respond in ways that protect what is revealed. A relationship that recognizes but does not respect a need reflects only partially. A whole relationship reflects accurately and responds with care.

The soul mirror holds you to the same standard you expect from others. You are responsible not only for honoring your own needs, but for honoring what is entrusted to you in someone else.

Outsourcing Our Needs

When you outsource your needs, you are not just giving others too much influence; you are refusing to reflect your own soul clearly. According to motivational speaker Jay Shetty, we must learn to motivate, validate, and even challenge ourselves without depending on others to do it for us. Otherwise, as he warns, "You'll always be waiting for someone else."

We haven't learned how to be a friend to ourselves, yet we expect others to show up in ways we don't or can't show up for ourselves. This is usually when we outsource our soul needs. In many cases, it's not only our sense of identity or value that we hand over to others, it's a unique but common soul need: **peace**.

True peace isn't something we chase; it's something we cultivate. It should be an internal state of being, not an external pursuit. When other people's moods or behaviors can disrupt your peace, it's a sign that your peace was never rooted within. It was built on their approval and responses.

Too often, we live like mirrors reflecting the energy, emotions, and attitudes of whoever stands before us. In doing so, we surrender our power. We unconsciously decide that others' perception of us matters more than our own, revealing a lack of self-containment and emotional boundaries.

That's why it's so important to guard access to yourself. Not everyone deserves full emotional or psychological access to you. Think about it: In a casual setting, a rude driver shouldn't have the power to ruin your day. Why give them that much control? On a deeper level, a love interest's harsh words or silence shouldn't make you question your worth or steal your peace.

Your peace is yours to protect. When you learn to center it within yourself, you stop living at the mercy of other people's moods, choices, and validation and start living from a place of grounded self-approval and wholeness.

Looking in the Soul Mirror

A clear mirror does more than reveal needs; it invites response. Once a need is seen, it must be named and expressed if it is to be honored. Thus, it is not always the relationship that is unfulfilling. Sometimes it is the absence of honest communication about our needs. Many fear that setting a boundary might cost them connection, yet unspoken needs often do more damage than honesty ever could. That is why we must continue looking in the soul mirror, noticing what our soul reflects in real time and responding with wisdom rather than fear.

Soul intelligence requires more than insight; it requires expression. When we ignore what truth, love, and faith are signaling, we distort the reflection and call the distortion "peace." We shrink ourselves and overtime feel empty because none of our soul needs are being addressed. Meanwhile, others may feel as if they have expressed their needs, but their attempts are clearly ineffective. These are unhealthy ways to communicate our needs:

- Silence
- Denial
- Ultimatums
- Blame

Many relationship breakdowns aren't caused by a lack of love but by unspoken or misunderstood needs. Research on attachment and emotional literacy shows that unmet needs are often the root of conflict. When people don't know how to unselfishly say, "I need," they tend to resort to criticism, control, or withdrawal, which are behaviors that create distance instead of understanding.

Communication scholar Marshall Rosenberg, in his model of Nonviolent Communication (NVC), observed that every form of negative expression – anger, blame or silence – masks an unmet need (Rosenberg 2003). Behind every complaint is a cry for connection, belonging or respect. For example, "You never listen to me" might really mean, *"I need to feel heard and valued."*

Rosenberg's process begins with four simple steps:

1. **Observation:** Describe what you see or hear without judgment.
2. **Feeling:** Name how it makes you feel.
3. **Need:** Identify the deeper need underneath the feeling.
4. **Request:** Express what would help meet that need constructively.

Instead of saying, "You're always distracted," a whole communicator might say,

"When you look at your phone while I'm talking, I feel unseen. I need to know our moments together matter. Could we take a few minutes just for us?"

Nonviolent Communication is one way we polish the mirror. It teaches us to separate observation from accusation and need from blame, so that what is reflected can be honored rather than distorted. Keep in mind, the soul mirror does two things at once: it reveals what your soul is signaling, and it exposes how clearly you and others are reflecting and responding to those signals. Sometimes the distortion is external. Sometimes it is internal.

(?) When something feels off:

1. What is my soul signaling right now?
2. Am I responding to that signal with honesty and care, and is the other person capable of doing the same?

The Childlike Mirror of Soul Needs

Soul intelligence is the discipline of reading your soul mirror in motion, noticing what truth, love, and faith are signaling in the moment and responding with honesty and courage. Children do this intuitively, displaying soul needs in their purest form. They love freely, tell the truth plainly, and trust instinctively. As we grow up, we learn protective habits, filtering truth to avoid rejection, rationing love by worthiness, and losing faith to fear. The goal isn't to be *childish*, but rather, it's to reclaim a childlike clarity about what the soul requires. Use this lens to read your soul mirror and act wisely:

- **LOVE (belonging/care)**
  Childlike expression: spontaneous affection, quick repair ("Can we play again?")
  Adult practice: timely repair attempts, warmth in tone, consistent bids for connection.
- **TRUTH (reality/integrity)**
  Childlike expression: unvarnished honesty ("I don't like that.")
  Adult practice: clear requests, direct updates, naming limits without shaming
- **FAITH (trust/meaning/hope)**
  Childlike expression: trying again without overthinking; expectation of good ("I believe in it.")
  Adult practice: courageous attempts, measured risk, shared vision rituals (weekly prayer, gratitude, mission review)

Children also display unique soul needs with stunning simplicity. In environments that welcome expression, their purpose, personality, and perspective (PPP) surface through play, questions, and requests. Some speak needs verbally; others "say" them through affection, body language, or gifts. Every action signals more-or-less of something: affection, affirmation, certain activities, or specific experiences. Those signals are early expressions of talent, traits, and time (TTT), the resources every soul uses to thrive.

Matthew 18:1–4 invites a return to childlike qualities of joy, forgiveness, humility, surrender, and trust. This is not about being childish but remembering what the soul has always required: Love, Truth, and Faith. When we learn to read these needs in children, we become better at recognizing and honoring them in adults, beginning with ourselves.

Childlike ≠ naive. It means needs are named simply and pursued consistently without manipulation or performances for approval.

Mapping to the Soul Needs

- TLF (universals): Children show love, truth and faith with immediacy.
- PPP (shape): A child's purpose, personality, perspective already peek through play and preferences.
- TTT (resources): Their talent, traits, time show up as natural interests, sensitivities, and rhythms. Adults still have these; they're just layered under social armor.

Childlike expression → Adult application

The chart below demonstrates how simple, childlike clarity becomes mature communication when guided by truth, love, and faith. This is how the soul mirror moves from insight to action.

Childlike Expression	Adult Application (Soul Mirror cue)	TLF Core	TTT Resource
"I'm sad."	"I feel hurt; I need reassurance today." (name it)	Love + Truth	Trait: sensitivity
"Play with me?"	"Can we set aside an hour tonight just for us?" (request it)	Love	Time: shared hour
"Watch this!"	"I need my work to be seen and appreciated this week." (affirmation)	Love + Truth	Talent: contribution
"Again!"	"Let's try that repair conversation once more." (persevere)	Faith	Trait: persistence

The difference between childlike expression and adult application is not the need itself. The need remains the same. What changes is the responsibility taken in expressing it.

Soul Intelligence is essentially childlike clarity applied with adult wisdom: TLF tells you ***what*** the soul needs; PPP×TTT shows you ***how*** to meet it in real life.

To ensure greater understanding and integration of Soul Intelligence, complete the Childlike Expressions Exercise in the workbook. Remember, mastery occurs when insight meets practice.

Children do not complicate their needs; they express them. What complicates us as adults is not intelligence, but ego. We fear that honesty will cost us control, dignity or connection. Yet it is often our refusal to speak plainly that erodes intimacy.

Adults don't fail at communication because they lack vocabulary. They fail because:

- Ego resists vulnerability
- Fear resists rejection
- Pride resists exposure
- Control resists dependence

Soul-Intelligence "mini-rule"

If a need cannot be expressed simply, it will eventually be expressed defensively. Use this "soul intelligence mini-rule" to help:

Say it simple. Say it soon. Say it with soul.
(Simple = childlike clarity. Soon = before resentment. Soul = TLF-aligned.)

Here are some example relationship repair scripts using the mini-rule:

- **Truth + Love (naming + warmth):**
  "I'm realizing I feel tense and a bit unseen (truth). I'd love ten minutes of eye-to-eye check-in after dinner (love). Can we do that tonight at 7:30?"
- **Faith + Truth (courage + clarity):**
  "This is hard to say (faith), but I need direct updates when plans shift (truth). If plans change after 5 p.m., please text me the same day."

Whole relationships are not built on impressive language or emotional strategy. They are built on honest, courageous expression and a willingness to respond with care. When two adults can speak with childlike clarity and listen with mature restraint, intimacy becomes safe.

Soul intelligence restores what ego complicates. It teaches you to read your soul mirror in motion and to respond with alignment. Sometimes alignment looks like saying what you feel clearly. Sometimes it looks like setting a boundary without hostility. Sometimes it looks like walking away without resentment. In simple terms, soul intelligence means responding with honesty and courage instead of fear and performance.

Whole love does not eliminate needs. It expresses them responsibly. As you move forward, remember: You are not learning to become someone new. You are learning to express who you already are truthfully, steadily, and without self-abandonment.

Whole, Mature Love

Soul Intelligence is the mature expression of love, the ability to perceive the deeper truth beneath a person's behavior and respond with wisdom instead of woundedness. It is the integration of everything the soul has learned: acknowledgement of your needs, understanding of your partner's needs, and the discernment to move in a way that protects the connection rather than endangers it.

Where discernment gives you clarity, Soul Intelligence gives you capability. It is love with direction. Love with understanding. Love with purpose. Love with accuracy. It is the wisdom to know *how* to love someone according to their soul, not simply according to your habits, your history, or your assumption of what love should look like.

Soul Intelligence allows you to:

- hear the need behind the words
- see the wound behind the reaction
- honor the heart beneath the fear
- protect the bond during conflict
- serve without self-abandonment
- love without losing yourself

When you practice Soul Intelligence, you stop demanding perfection and start practicing presence. You stop reacting to pain and start responding to need. You stop fighting your partner and start fighting for the connection. You stop assuming and start attuning. This is the maturity that transforms relationships.

Soul Intelligence elevates love from emotion to intention; from chemistry to connection; from desire to devotion; and from effort to understanding. It is the spiritual skill that allows two imperfect souls to love each other *wisely*, *humbly*, and *whole*. Whether you are seeking a Whole Relationship or restoring one, soul intelligence changes how you choose and how you respond. It teaches you to look beyond chemistry, beyond conflict, and beyond comfort and to build connection on what nourishes the soul.

> *"Soul intelligence is learning to read your soul mirror in motion."*

Now that you understand the internal soul intelligence required to love well, you are ready to learn the **five external expressions** that make connection safe, stable, and sacred. These expressions form the T.O.R.C.H. of Love, the relational language of a Whole Relationship. Together, they illuminate the path from discernment to devotion, from internal clarity to interpersonal connection, and from soul to soul.

PART III REVIEW: THE SOUL ESSENTIALS

Love begins in the soul. In Part III, you uncovered the blueprint of your inner life: the universal needs (truth, love, and faith) that ground every human heart and the unique design (purpose, personality and perspective) that shape how those needs are expressed (talents, traits, and time).

You examined:

- why unmet needs distort decisions,
- how to distinguish desire from deficiency,
- and what it means to serve your soul instead of starving it.

You walked through the four stages of maturity (Acknowledgment, Analysis, Actualization, and Attainment) and discovered that growth happens when needs are honored rather than hidden. This changes how you love.

When you understand your soul needs, you stop choosing from loneliness and start choosing from clarity. You stop reacting from deficiency and start responding from discernment. You become capable of expressing your needs without accusation and evaluating whether they are received with care.

Whole love requires soul intelligence: the ability to see your needs clearly, speak them honestly, and steward them wisely. Now that you understand your soul needs, love must move from awareness to expression in relating to others.

Before beginning Part IV, review the affirmations in ***Appendix E*** *that support your Soul Needs' expression and alignment. For journal prompts to explore your Soul's Identity, visit* ***Appendix F****.*

PART IV

THE T.O.R.C.H. OF LOVE

Loving Others Whole

11

CONNECTING TO OTHERS

Love is not proven by what we feel internally. It is revealed by how we show up for another person. A whole relationship forms when two people bring self-awareness, soul clarity, and a sense of responsibility into connection with each other.

Many people long for connection but struggle to sustain it because they confuse *chemistry* with *closeness*. Chemistry draws you together; connection keeps you together. True connection is built on safety, truth, and mutual respect, the very foundations of a whole relationship.

Connection, therefore, is not chemistry. It is not attraction or compatibility alone. Connection is the practice of showing up with honesty, care, and humility so that both people feel safe enough to be fully themselves. This is where the **TORCH of Love** becomes essential.

In this part of the book, we explore what it truly means to love others wholly through the five relational practices (flames) of TORCH:

- **T** — **Trust**: the foundation of safe connection
  O — **Openness**: the language of vulnerability
  R — **Respect**: seeing the sacred in others
  C — **Communication**: the bridge to understanding
  H — **Humility**: the hidden strength of love

Together, these five qualities keep love illuminated, much like a torch lighting a path in darkness. When one flame dims, the whole connection weakens, but when all five burn together, they illuminate a connection built on truth, compassion, and shared growth. Thus, they must be practiced consistently, so a connection remains safe and sustaining.

Before we explore these five flames, we must first understand **what blocks connection**, the *idols* we unknowingly serve that keep us from authentic intimacy.

Surrendering Our Idols

Our *soul needs* are divine in origin, so they are sacred, not selfish. God placed them within us so that we might seek Him, not so that we might seek substitutes. Yet when these needs go unmet, we often turn to people, possessions or patterns to fill the void. We start looking for peace outside of the One who gives it. That's when our needs transform into **attachments**, and those attachments, if left unchecked, become **idols**. What begins as a search for connection turns into dependence on something or someone incapable of satisfying the soul. To experience love as God designed, we must learn to surrender those false sources of fulfillment.

Wholeness requires surrender, yet surrender is one of the hardest acts of love we will ever perform. Before we can embody the TORCH of Love we must release what we hold above God: idols. An idol is not always a literal statue. It is anything God desires that we are unwilling to give Him, anything we cannot release or allow Him to direct. Sometimes our idols are people, possessions, or even our own emotions.

When we make our **feelings** the final authority, we begin to worship them as truth. We let pain, pride, anger or fear dictate our responses instead of faith. In doing so, our soul needs for safety, love, purpose, belonging, and growth become distorted. We chase counterfeit comfort rather than divine connection.

We may even make idols out of our children, our relationships or the idea of being in control. For instance, in making our *children* idols, we fear surrendering them completely to God's care. We think we're protecting them, but often we're preventing God from working in their lives as He desires. Similarly, our need to control, be right, or protect ourselves can function as both **emotional** *and* **psychological idols**, depending on what drives them.

- **Emotional idols** are formed when our **feelings** become the authority. For example, when fear, anger, or insecurity guide our choices, we begin to worship the feeling itself, trying to appease it or avoid it at all costs. We're driven by emotion rather than led by faith.

  → "I can't let go because I'm afraid."
  → "I have to prove I'm right to feel safe."

- **Psychological idols** emerge when our **mindset or belief system** becomes rigid and self-protective. These are strongholds of the *ego*: needing to control outcomes, to be seen as right or to avoid vulnerability.

They're rooted in patterns of thought that elevate self-preservation over surrender.

→ "If I'm not in control, I'll be hurt again."
→ "If I admit I'm wrong, I'll lose respect."

In essence, emotional idols are what we *feel compelled* by, while psychological idols are what we *justify and rationalize* to maintain control. In other words, emotional idols control our reactions, while psychological idols defend our beliefs. Both block the flow of love because they keep us centered on *self-protection* instead of *Spirit direction.* Wholeness requires surrendering both our emotional attachments and our psychological defenses so that love can move freely through us to others.

When we refuse to surrender these strongholds, our hearts harden, and the flow of love through the TORCH is blocked. Without surrender, we cannot trust. Without trust, we cannot respect. Without respect, communication collapses, and connection becomes impossible.

To surrender is to realign, not to lose. God will never ask us to release something without redeeming it through purpose. Surrender simply acknowledges that He is the Source, not our emotions, not other people, and not our self-protection.

True wholeness begins when we can say, *"Lord, You can have all of it – my fears, my attachments, my career, my children, my feelings, my control."* Only then can love flow freely through us and to others.

As you begin applying these principles to relationships, remember: insight without safety can create conflict rather than connection. The workbook includes communication and repair language designed to support practice without escalation. Use it before difficult conversations, not after.

Understanding How to Connect Effectively

We make room for genuine relationship connection when we surrender our idols, such as our need to control, be right or protect ourselves. Surrender softens the heart and clears the noise of pride, fear, and unmet needs, allowing love to flow freely again. Only then can we meet others, not from our wounds but from our wholeness. This is where connection begins: when the barriers fall and we are safe enough within ourselves to make others feel safe with us.

When someone is hurting, the human heart shuts its doors. Fear, shame, or disappointment can make even the most loving words sound like noise. That's why the first principle of Christ-like communication is to **connect before you communicate** in order to build a bridge of safety strong enough to carry the weight of truth. This is why connection must occur before correction, creating a sense of safety first. Essentially, before love can be spoken, it must be *felt.*

1. Why Connection Comes First

Communication is about information; connection is about *safety*. If the person you're speaking with doesn't feel safe, their nervous system is in defense, not dialogue. Before you can *be heard*, you must *be trusted*. Connection says: *You matter more than the message right now.*

Jesus modeled this

- He touched the leper before speaking a word of healing.
- He wept with Mary and Martha before raising Lazarus.
- He sat at tables with sinners before teaching them about the kingdom.

Each act communicated the same message, *"You are safe with me."*

2. What Connection Looks Like

Verbal ways to connect:

- "I can tell this has been really painful for you."
- "You don't have to explain everything right now; I just want to understand."
- "Before we talk about what happened, I want you to know I care about you."
- "I'm not here to judge; I just want us to listen to each other."
- "Would you like me to just listen right now or do you want my thoughts?"

These short statements lower emotional temperature. They communicate humility (H), respect (R), and openness (O), which are three TORCH pillars that prepare the heart for truth.

Nonverbal ways to connect:

- Keep your **voice steady and low**, even if emotions rise.
- **Soften your eyes**; look with compassion, not interrogation.
- **Lean slightly forward** or nod to show engagement without intrusion.
- **Pause before responding**, as silence can be healing.
- **Uncross your arms** and relax your shoulders. Openness of body mirrors openness of heart.
- **Avoid multitasking**, so put the phone down, and get rid of distractions. Attention itself communicates worth.

Small cues like these tell a wounded person, *"You're not in danger here."* Only then can deeper honesty follow.

3. Connection Before Correction

It's tempting to rush into fixing, explaining or defending. However, premature correction can feel like rejection.

Connection is not agreement; it's alignment with compassion. You can hold someone accountable without making them feel disposable. Try saying:

- "I want to talk about what hurt me but not in a way that makes you feel attacked. Can we take a breath first?"
- "There's something I need to be honest about, but I want to make sure you feel safe hearing it."

This turns confrontation into collaboration, or truth shared *with* someone, not *at* them.

4. The Spiritual Posture

Connecting before communicating reflects God's own rhythm: *presence before proclamation*.

When the Father called to Adam, He didn't start with blame. He started with connection: "Where are you?" (Genesis 3:9). That question wasn't for information; it was an invitation to safety and self-awareness.

We do the same when we ask, gently, "Where are you right now?" or "What are you feeling underneath that?" This invites the person out of hiding and into honesty.

5. The TORCH in Action

- **T — Trust:** I will be steady even if you're stormy.
- **O — Openness:** I will listen for what's said and unsaid.
- **R — Respect:** I will protect your dignity while we discuss truth.
- **C — Communication:** I will speak clearly but calmly.
- **H — Humility:** I know healing takes time and grace.

When we connect before we communicate, broken people experience love before language. Only then can truth land softly enough to do its healing work.

> *"Connection is not chemistry. It is the courage to show up honestly so another soul can safely do the same."*

TORCH Language

Once we surrender what stands between us and God, including our idols, attachments, and self-protective patterns, we become open channels of love. That surrender clears the interference that keeps us from *hearing*, *speaking*, and *receiving* love rightly, or wholly.

Now, love must be expressed. This is where the TORCH of Love becomes our guide. TORCH is both a posture and a practice, a language of the soul that teaches us how to love as Christ loved: with trust, openness, respect, communication, and humility. In practical terms, TORCH language is how whole people speak when they want connection instead of control. These are not mere relational skills; they are spiritual disciplines that reflect the condition of our hearts.

The more we surrender, the more fluently we speak this language and connect with others. When we trust, we release control. When we are open, we surrender fear. When we show respect, we let go of pride. When we communicate with truth and compassion, we silence shame. When we express humility, we surrender the need to protect our pain while recognizing others'.

TORCH language is how surrendered, whole people love – with humility, honesty, and hope that invites others into connection. Here are some conversational examples of each TORCH element:

Trust

"You can rely on me."

"Don't worry."

"I won't let you down."

"I give you my word."

Openness

"I need…"

"I think..."

"I feel..."

"I want..." or "I don't want…"

Respect

"What do you need from me?"

"I did this for you."

"I didn't do it because I knew you wouldn't like it."

"I took your suggestion."

Communication

"Let's talk."

"I'm listening."

"Let me explain."

"You should know…"

Humility

"I'm sorry."

"It's my fault."

"What do you think?"

"I don't know."

The TORCH of Love is not a formula to master but a language to live. It translates divine love into daily action, transforming how we relate to God, to others, and to ourselves. As we will explore next, "trust" is the first word in that language. Only when connection becomes intentional can trust begin to grow.

For a complete reference chart of TORCH language, see ***Appendix C****.*

12

TRUST: THE FOUNDATION OF SAFE CONNECTION

Trust is the foundation of any whole relationship. It is the first flame of love and the steady light that keeps every other flame alive. Trust requires surrender, the willingness to release control and allow reliability to replace fear. It begins with a promise that asserts, *"You can rely on me."* It's not built through grand gestures but through small, consistent acts of reliability. Every time you show up, keep your word, tell the truth, or admit a mistake, you place another brick in the foundation of safety.

Gottman calls this "emotional attunement," the ability to notice, respond, and follow through on your partner's needs and bids for connection. These small moments, such as returning a text, remembering a detail or offering reassurance, create emotional security over time. The opposite is also true: when these moments are ignored, dismissed, or broken by dishonesty, the foundation begins to crack.

Spiritually, trust is born from *truthfulness* and *faithfulness*, two qualities that reflect the character of God Himself. Just as faith is the belief that God will do what He says, relational trust grows from the same soil of consistency, integrity, and humility. Love without trust is like fire without oxygen; it cannot last. Whether spiritual or natural, trust requires faith in God's character and a willingness to believe the best about others. When we trust, we surrender control and rest in divine order rather than human certainty.

How Trust Is Built

Trust is built in layers, not leaps. It forms through patterns of dependability that tell the other person, *"You are safe here."*

Below are the key ingredients that cultivate trust in any relationship:

- **Consistency:** Keeping your word, showing up when you say you will, and maintaining steady behavior over time.
- **Transparency:** Being honest about your intentions, mistakes, and limitations. Secrets may protect your comfort, but they destroy connection.
- **Accountability:** Taking responsibility when your actions cause harm. A sincere "I was wrong" repairs more than defensiveness ever can.
- **Empathy:** Listening to understand, not to defend. Empathy communicates, "Your feelings matter to me."
- **Boundaries:** Respecting your partner's limits and maintaining your own. Without boundaries, trust collapses under emotional chaos or control.

Trust grows strongest when both people feel emotionally *seen* and spiritually *safe.*

How Trust Is Broken

Trust rarely shatters all at once; it erodes in moments such as with a forgotten promise, a half-truth, or a defensive tone. These small fractures accumulate. The most common ways trust is broken include:

- **Dishonesty or deception** — withholding truth, lying by omission, or pretending.
- **Neglect or emotional absence** — failing to be present when the other person needs you most.
- **Disrespect** — dismissing feelings, mocking vulnerability, or betraying confidences.
- **Control and manipulation** — using guilt, power, or fear to get compliance instead of consent.

When trust is broken, the natural response is *protection.* The offended person retreats, creating emotional distance to avoid future pain. Healing cannot happen until both people acknowledge the rupture and commit to repair, not blame.

How Trust Is Rebuilt

Rebuilding trust is a process of restoration, not performance. It takes time, transparency, and truth. The one who broke the trust must be patient with the other's fear, just as the one who was hurt must be willing to see change, not perfection.

Rebuilding trust is slower than breaking it. Restoration happens through repeated proof of reliability. Here are the guiding steps:

- **Acknowledge the wound**. Healing begins with honesty: "I hurt you." Pretending it didn't happen deepens the injury.
- **Listen without defending**. Allow the other person to express their pain fully without minimizing or redirecting.
- **Show consistent change**. Apologies open the door, but reliability keeps it open. Let your actions speak more than your promises.
- **Create new boundaries**. Rebuilding trust sometimes means redefining what safety looks like together.
- **Invite accountability**. Allow time, truth, and even others (counselors, mentors, or faith leaders) to hold the process accountable.

Forgiveness and trust are related but not identical. Forgiveness is a decision of the heart; trust is the fruit of consistent action. You can forgive instantly, but trust must be earned over time.

Recognizing Reliability vs. Control

Reliability builds connection; control destroys it.

- **A reliable person acts out of** *love***:** "I want to protect and support you."
- **A controlling person acts out of** *fear***:** "I need to manage you to feel secure."

Control often disguises itself as care:

- "I'm just checking in."
- "I know what's best for you."
- "I only do this because I love you."

However, control is not protection, it's possession. Reliability, on the other hand, respects autonomy. It says, *"You can rely on me, but you are still free."*

Healthy trust allows both partners to breathe, move and grow. It creates safety without suffocation. When trust is mature, love no longer fears freedom. It celebrates it.

> *"Trust is not built in grand promises but in small, consistent proofs of reliability."*

Trust Principle at Work

Trust is the first flame of the TORCH, and it fuels every principle that follows. When trust burns steadily, love has a solid foundation on which to flourish. Without it, even good intentions feel unstable.

Trust is built through consistency. Following through on what you say you will do communicates reliability, which calms fear and creates emotional safety. Over time, this steadiness allows confidence to grow. When trust is broken, however, confidence erodes, fear takes its place, and safety dissolves, not because love disappears, but because uncertainty takes over.

Wholeness requires trust on three levels. It asks us to trust God, believing that He does not remove anything from our lives without redeeming it for our good and His purpose. It also asks us to trust others wisely, extending reliability and openness where it is earned. Finally, it requires trust in ourselves, the confidence that we can discern truth, honor our boundaries, and respond with integrity. When these forms of trust work together, love is no longer driven by fear of loss but anchored in alignment and growth.

As you work through Part IV, complete the T.O.R.C.H. of Love pages in the workbook to sharpen your understanding and usage. Integration happens when insight meets practice, and trust is something that needs consistent training.

13

OPENNESS: THE LANGUAGE OF VULNERABILITY

Openness is the posture of a surrendered heart. It invites vulnerability without fear, allowing us to be seen as we are. Without openness, love cannot breathe.

Vulnerability is consciously choosing not to hide your emotions or desires from others. It is the willingness to express your thoughts, feelings, and needs honestly rather than protecting yourself through silence or performance. This level of honesty requires courage and trust. It's not recklessness, but reverence for truth. When we are open, we offer others a genuine invitation into who we are, our being.

In relationships, that invitation often appears as what relationship researcher Dr. John Gottman calls a *bid for connection*. Every "How was your day?" or gentle touch on the shoulder is a way of saying, *"See me. Hear me. Be with me."*

Our openness determines how we send and receive these bids. When our hearts are guarded, we may overlook or minimize them. When we are emotionally available, we recognize them as opportunities for intimacy and growth.

Not every gesture of attention is a true bid, however. Some interactions resemble *bids* but lack depth or follow-through. These are what psychologists and attachment theorists describe as *breadcrumbs.* A breadcrumb mimics connection while keeping vulnerability safely out of reach.

Learning to discern a genuine bid from a breadcrumb is essential to sustaining whole relationships. It allows us to respond with wisdom, keeping our hearts open without being misled by inconsistency or emotional avoidance.

Genuine Bids for Connection

A *bid* is any small action or signal meant to connect with someone (Gottman & DeClaire, 2001). It's an invitation to engage emotionally, mentally, or physically. A genuine bid, however, carries real *intention and openness*. It's not about control, reassurance or ego maintenance.

Signs it's a genuine bid:

- **Emotional sincerity**: There's authentic interest or warmth behind it ("How was your day?" because they *want to* know).
- **Availability for response**: They're ready for whatever comes back, including conversation, closeness or even vulnerability.
- **Consistency**: They make bids regularly, not just when they fear losing you.
- **Follow-through**: If you respond positively, they stay engaged and deepen the interaction.
- **Shared benefit**: The bid nourishes both people. It's about mutual connection, not managing distance.
- **Embodied presence**: Tone, timing, and energy feel grounded, not anxious or transactional.

Breadcrumbs

A *breadcrumb* mimics a bid, but it's actually a defensive move, a way to maintain some connection without risking real intimacy. It's self-protective, not co-creative.

Signs it's a breadcrumb:

- **Low vulnerability**: It's vague or emotionally empty ("Hey," "Miss ya," "How's life?" with no follow-up).
- **Poor follow-through**: When you respond warmly, they withdraw or don't deepen the exchange.
- **Timing control**: It comes when they sense you detaching, only meant to pull you back in.
- **Inconsistency**: The rhythm feels unpredictable, so you can't trust when they'll reach out.
- **Emotionally one-sided**: It calms *their* anxiety about closeness or abandonment, but it leaves you unfulfilled.
- **Avoidance of growth**: The connection doesn't progress; it resets the same shallow cycle.

Breakdown

	Genuine Bid	Breadcrumb
Intention	To connect and engage	To manage distance or maintain control
Emotional depth	Authentic, open	Shallow, self-protective
Response to reciprocation	Leans in	Pulls back
Consistency	Regular and reliable	Sporadic or reactive
Outcome	Builds intimacy	Sustains confusion

 Here's a simple litmus test:

After their action, do you feel **closer**, more grounded, and seen or **confused**, anxious, and searching for meaning? That feeling usually tells you whether it was a *bid* or a *breadcrumb.*

Recognizing a bid for connection requires presence and emotional courage. Researcher and author Brené Brown notes that we often "armor up" when we fear rejection or judgment. That armor – perfectionism, control, emotional detachment – blocks our capacity to see or respond to the small invitations for closeness that others offer. To stay open to bids, we must remove the armor and become vulnerable. Vulnerability allows us to "turn toward" others, as Gottman recommends, rather than away, trusting that intimacy is worth the risk of being hurt.

Vulnerability as Revelation

Vulnerability draws out truth, providing revelation. It exposes truth, both in you and in the one to whom you're relating. If you're with someone who is emotionally available, your openness becomes an invitation to deeper intimacy. It empowers the other person to be expressive in return. For instance, your willingness to say, *"I was thinking about you,"* might inspire them to share something they were hesitant to admit. Vulnerability invites reciprocity.

If the person you're dealing with isn't capable of that kind of depth, your vulnerability will reveal that too. Their lack of response or their defensiveness tells you everything you need to know. In this way, vulnerability never works against you. Whether it opens someone's heart or exposes their absence, it always brings clarity. Thus, vulnerability is a soul truth that triggers soul truth in another person.

When you allow yourself to be emotionally open, you're not just sharing your heart; you're revealing the *spiritual temperature* of the connection. Many people protect themselves with emotional shields, including walls of silence, sarcasm, or avoidance, believing they're guarding their hearts from rejection. Those same walls also block connection. It's the paradox of protection: In trying to avoid pain, we also shut out joy.

Whole love requires the courage to risk being seen. Vulnerability is that risk. It is faith in action, the belief that openness will either deepen a bond or deliver the truth you need to move on. In either case, you win, because you've chosen courage over comfort and truth over pretense.

> *"Vulnerability never works against you. It either deepens connection or reveals its absence."*

Relearning How to Speak Your Truth

Whole relationships rely on simple, honest language. Meanwhile, most of us were never taught how to speak the language of emotional honesty. We learned how to communicate needs indirectly through hints, moods or withdrawal because being transparent once felt unsafe. Openness, therefore, is a relearning process: rediscovering how to voice our truth in ways that build intimacy instead of fear.

To be open in a whole relationship is to relearn how to speak with both honesty and humility. Speaking your truth doesn't mean saying everything you think; it means saying what matters most in a way that nurtures connection rather than wounds it.

Whole communication starts with *ownership*. Thus, you begin communication with "I" rather than "You." For instance:

- "I think…" expresses perspective without presumption.
- "I feel…" names emotion without accusation.
- "I want…" reveals desire without demand.
- "I need…" communicates vulnerability and dependency.

These simple phrases are building blocks for emotional clarity. They turn vulnerability into strength by aligning language with self-awareness. Instead of saying, "You make me feel ignored," try, "I feel unseen when we don't connect."

The first blames; the second invites understanding.

"I need" is often the hardest phrase to say because it exposes our humanity. Yet in whole relationships, expressing need is wisdom, not weakness. It invites trust rather than assumption. When you can articulate your needs clearly, you give others the opportunity to respond with love rather than guess through fear.

When we speak our truth from wholeness, we stop trying to control outcomes and start cultivating understanding. We no longer demand to be heard; we invite others to listen. We replace criticism with clarity, sarcasm with sincerity, and pride with presence. When spoken with humility, even uncomfortable truths can become gateways to deeper connection. This allows truth to be a bridge rather than a weapon.

Speaking your truth, then, is not merely communication, it's communion. It is the meeting place where self-awareness meets surrender, and where love learns to listen back.

Why Honesty Without Empathy Still Wounds

Honesty without empathy is brutality. Words can tell the truth and still break the heart if they're not wrapped in compassion.

Many people mistake bluntness for authenticity, believing that "keeping it real" gives them permission to disregard gentleness and kindness. However, whole love requires more than raw truth. It requires redemptive truth.

Empathy transforms honesty into healing. It allows you to express what is real without shaming what is tender. Saying, *"This hurt me, but I still care,"* is far more powerful than, *"You always hurt me."* One invites closeness; the other provokes defense.

Wholeness teaches us that truth and love are not opposites; they are allies. The Apostle Paul wrote that we must "speak the truth in love," because truth without love divides, while love without truth deceives. Together, they restore.

When honesty is delivered with empathy, vulnerability becomes safe again. It shows that openness is not weakness; it's wisdom guided by grace

The Cost of Emotional Hiding

Emotional hiding is the quiet killer of intimacy. It begins subtly by silencing a thought here or withholding a feeling there, until the relationship becomes polite but distant.

We hide to avoid rejection, judgment or loss, but the cost of hiding is always higher than the risk of honesty. Hiding may protect our image or feelings, but it starves intimacy. Every time you suppress your truth to avoid discomfort, you trade authenticity for approval. Approval, no matter how comforting, cannot sustain love.

Whole love requires showing up fully, even when it's messy. It doesn't demand that you have it all together. It only asks that you be real. Emotional transparency builds trust; concealment builds walls. Wholeness involves *naming needs without shame* and *expressing them without entitlement.* That's what differentiates a whole relationship from a codependent one.

When you stop hiding, you give others permission to be authentic too. Vulnerability becomes contagious, and connection becomes effortless. Love flourishes in the light of honesty.

If you learned early that honesty was unsafe, pause here. In your journal, explore what you were protecting yourself from when you learned to hide.

Openness as an Act of Faith

Openness is an act of faith. It's believing that truth will set you free, even if it first makes you uncomfortable. It's trusting that the right hearts will handle your transparency with care, and that even if they don't, God will heal what honesty reveals.

When we dare to be open, we step into the sacred territory of whole love, a love that doesn't demand perfection, only presence.

Openness is what makes respect possible. When we allow ourselves to be seen and choose to see others without judgment, we create space for reverence to take root. Respect begins where defensiveness ends – when we can honor another person's truth without fear or control. The next chapter explores this sacred exchange: how seeing the divine worth in others transforms the way we love, listen, and live in wholeness.

14

RESPECT: SEEING THE SACRED IN OTHERS

Respect is the recognition of divine worth in ourselves and in others. It is love made visible through consideration, empathy, and restraint. Respect honors boundaries, celebrates difference, and seeks understanding instead of dominance. It is the spiritual practice of seeing another person as God sees them: valuable, purposeful, and worthy of dignity.

In Chapter 5, we explored **self-respect**, how honoring your own design allows you to live from truth instead of fear. Now we turn outward, to the sacred art of respecting others. Whole relationships require both: knowing your worth *and* recognizing theirs.

So many times, we've heard that respect must be earned. That phrase usually arises when we feel hurt or disrespected, when trust has been broken or value ignored. Spiritually speaking, respect is not something another person must earn; it is something *we choose to give* because we understand that every human being bears the image of God.

To "see the sacred in the other" means to acknowledge that their soul has value even when their behavior doesn't. You can respect someone's humanity without endorsing their actions. In fact, setting boundaries is one of the highest forms of respect for both parties. It says, *"I value us enough not to let harm continue."*

Why Respect Matters

Respect is the soil where love grows. Without it, affection becomes manipulation, and commitment turns into control. Research from the Gottman Institute found that contempt, such as rolling the eyes, sarcasm, name-calling or dismissive tones, is the single strongest predictor of relationship failure. Contempt is the opposite of respect; it corrodes trust and intimacy until only resentment remains.

When respect is present, however, love feels safe. Partners can disagree without dishonoring each other. They can confront without condemning. Respect creates a climate of mutual regard where truth can be spoken and vulnerability received.

What Respect Looks Like

1. **Listening without interruption.** Giving someone space to speak communicates, *"Your voice matters."*
2. **Disagreeing without demeaning.** It's possible to challenge ideas while still affirming worth.
3. **Keeping confidences.** Protecting what is shared in trust is a sacred act of respect.
4. **Honoring boundaries.** Accepting "no" without punishment preserves emotional safety.
5. **Acknowledging effort.** Gratitude affirms the unseen work of love, or what the other person tries to do right.

Every act of respect, however small, says: *"I see you, and you matter."*

Reflection: A Mirror of Honor

Ask yourself:

- Do I speak to others with the same kindness I want to receive?
- When someone disagrees with me, do I listen to understand or to win?
- How do I respond when I feel disrespected: do I retaliate or recalibrate?

Respect is not passive; it is active recognition. It's how we protect the sacredness of love while allowing both people to remain whole.

How Respect Maintains Attraction and Affection

Respect doesn't just preserve peace; it sustains passion. It is the quiet fuel that keeps affection alive long after the initial spark has faded. When respect is mutual, both partners feel valued, heard, and free to show up authentically. That freedom is what keeps connection vibrant.

While love captures the heart, **respect holds it steady.** It tells your partner, *"You matter as you are, not just when you please me."* Research consistently shows that feeling respected is one of the strongest predictors of long-term relationship satisfaction.

A popular study by Jennifer Frei and Phillip Shaver found that respect is often a stronger determinant of relationship quality than love itself. In their work, participants reported that feeling respected created a deeper sense of safety, validation, and mutual regard, sometimes more sustaining than romantic affection alone. When partners felt disrespected, even consistent expressions of love couldn't repair the erosion of trust and emotional safety (Frei and Shaver 2002).

A 2024 study on respect dynamics further expanded this understanding, identifying two main forms of respect that shape relational commitment:

- **Status-based respect** — acknowledging a partner's abilities, strengths, and contributions.
- **Inclusion-based respect** — affirming their inherent belonging and equal value in the relationship.

Both types matter. When partners feel admired for who they are *and* assured they belong, their commitment deepens. The relationship becomes not just a partnership, but a sanctuary for self-expression.

As psychotherapist Esther Perel observes, desire and connection thrive not in ownership but in admiration. Perel suggests that we often confuse love with fusion, wanting to merge so completely that mystery disappears (Perel 2006). Yet it is respect that allows love to breathe. Perel reminds us that passion endures when we continue to see our partners as separate, complex beings when we respect their individuality instead of demanding sameness.

This mirrors spiritual truth: God's design for relationship was never about control or conformity but about co-creation: two souls choosing to honor each other's divine spark while growing in unity. In other words, **respect keeps the sacred space between two people intact.**

When respect fades, attraction dims. This is not because beauty disappears, but because resentment grows where admiration once lived. However, when respect is nurtured through appreciation, attentiveness, and humility, love remains magnetic, tender, and alive.

Practice: The "I See You" Exercise

Take a few minutes with your partner or a close friend to express one way you see and value them beyond what they *do* for you. For example:

- "I see how much care you put into your work."
- "I admire the patience you show with others."
- "I respect the way you hold to your values, even when it's hard."

If practiced regularly, this simple habit reshapes how you both experience love, transforming daily interactions into moments of mutual reverence.

> *"You can challenge someone's actions without diminishing their dignity."*

Additional guided exercises for building respect and appreciation can be found in the companion workbook.

Reverence as Relationship

Many believe that respect is simply good manners, but it is spiritual maturity in motion. When we honor the divine in another person, we participate in God's own love. Every act of respect becomes a form of worship, reminding us that people are not ours to control or correct, but souls to cherish and understand.

Seeing others as sacred restores balance to our relationships and humility to our hearts. It turns conflict into compassion and difference into discovery. In this way, respect is not just the foundation of healthy connection, it is a pathway to divine wholeness.

When we treat others with reverence, we align ourselves with the very nature of God. Ultimately, in honoring the divine in them, we strengthen the divine connection within ourselves. Keep in mind, respect opens the door, and communication walks us through it. When we honor the divine in another person, we create a safe space for truth to be spoken and heard. Words can only heal when they are carried on the current of respect. Without it, even the right message can feel like a wound. However, when love and reverence shape our tone, communication becomes sacred dialogue, a bridge that keeps hearts connected even when minds differ.

15

COMMUNICATION: THE BRIDGE TO UNDERSTANDING

Communication is the bridge that keeps love from drifting apart. It is the steady rhythm that carries connection from one heart to another. When it flows freely, relationships feel warm and alive, like the glow of a fire that keeps love illuminated. When communication falters, the fire dims, leaving both people standing in the dark, guessing at what the other feels.

You can have passion, purpose, and even shared faith, but without clear and compassionate communication, relationships struggle to remain connected. Words are like the sticks that feed the fire, each one placed intentionally, each one nurturing warmth. Neglect them, and even great love grows cold.

Poor communication is not just a relationship flaw; it's a form of emotional isolation. Silence can feel like rejection, defensiveness like disrespect, and assumptions like abandonment. Yet the opposite, speaking carelessly or without empathy, can wound just as deeply. Whole communication calls for balance: the courage to speak truth and the grace to speak it kindly.

- **Healthy communication** focuses on solving problems.
- **Whole communication** focuses on strengthening connection.

In a whole relationship, words are not weapons or shields; they are bridges. Whole communication reflects wholeness within the self: awareness of emotion, surrender of ego, and service to the soul of another. It is not reactive but responsive, not manipulative but mindful. A whole communicator listens as much to the heart as to the words, understanding that every conversation is an opportunity to heal or to harm.

When we communicate from wholeness, we don't speak to win. Instead, we speak to *understand*. We don't listen to reply; we listen to *restore*. We don't withhold truth; we share it in a way that builds trust instead of breaking it.

Whole communication is not about saying everything. It's about saying what matters in a way that multiplies grace.

Replacing Assumption with Articulation

Most relationships don't fall apart from lack of love. They fracture under the weight of unspoken expectations. We assume others can read what we need, feel what we feel, or understand what we meant. However, assumption is not connection; it's imagination. Whole relationships replace guessing with clarity. The moment we replace assumption with articulation, we begin to bridge the gap between intention and understanding.

Whole communication requires transparency. It's not enough to *feel* deeply. You must also *express* clearly. A whole communicator doesn't expect their partner to guess what's wrong or right. They practice truth-telling that is honest but not harsh, direct but not domineering.

Think of articulation as the act of giving love direction. Feelings without expression can't find their way to another heart. When you can name what's happening inside you, you invite the other person into your inner world instead of making them try to decode it.

Psychologist Sue Johnson reminds us that most arguments are not about the surface issue, such as money, time or chores, but about emotional safety underneath (Johnson 2008). When someone snaps, withdraws, or shuts down, they're rarely saying, *"I don't care."* More often, they're saying, *"I feel disconnected."* Assumption interprets these moments as attack or rejection; articulation transforms them into opportunities for intimacy.

To communicate from wholeness, start by naming your inner truth with both humility and courage. Instead of assuming your partner knows why you're upset, you might say:

"When we talk about this and you look away, I feel unseen."

"When you step back instead of answering, I start to worry that I've done something wrong."

Notice that whole articulation begins with **self-awareness**, not accusation. It doesn't demand that the other person change; it invites them to understand.

Whole communicators use language that connects, not condemns. For example:

- They replace "You never…" with "I feel…"
- They replace "You should know…" with "Let me share what's happening inside me."

- They replace "Forget it" with "This matters to me, so can we talk about it?"

It's not always easy, but it's holy work. Speaking from truth rather than tension allows love to stay grounded in respect. When you articulate rather than assume, you give grace room to enter the conversation. Articulation is how love learns to speak fluently.

The Three Modes of Communication: Verbal, Nonverbal, and Spiritual

Words may carry meaning, but presence carries truth. Communication happens in more ways than speech. It is the full expression of what we think, feel, and believe. Whole communication integrates three modes: **verbal, non-verbal**, and **spiritual**. Each one reveals a different layer of love's language.

1. Verbal Communication — Speaking with Integrity

Verbal communication is the most obvious and often the most misleading form. We tend to believe what people say, but the power of words depends on the spirit in which they are spoken. Wholeness requires speaking from authenticity, not impulse.

The goal of verbal communication in a whole relationship isn't to be eloquent; it's to be *aligned*. When your words match your values, tone, and actions, you create safety. When they don't, you create confusion.

Whole communication doesn't just say what is true. It says it *truthfully*. Words of wholeness are clear but compassionate, honest but humble. They aim to clarify, not to control. They restore dignity rather than demand submission. Even difficult truths can become healing when spoken in love.

2. Nonverbal Communication — The Language of Presence

As relationship researcher Sue Johnson notes in *Hold Me Tight*, emotional connection is sustained less by words and more by *responsiveness*, the tone of voice, the softness of a look, the comfort of proximity (Johnson 2008). These subtle signals say, *"You matter,"* long before any words do.

Research on communication confirms this pattern. Psychologist Albert Mehrabian's well-known "7–38–55 rule" suggested that when verbal and nonverbal messages conflict, **7 percent of meaning** is conveyed **through words**, **38 percent through tone of voice**, and **55 percent through facial expressions and body language** (Mehrabian 1971). Later analyses, such as those by communication educators, estimated that in typical interactions, approximately 60 percent of meaning is communicated nonverbally (Burgoon and Bacue 2003). When vocal tone and body language contradict our words, people typically believe what they *see*, not what they *hear.*

Whole communication therefore means **being present in your presence.** Here are some examples:

- It's maintaining gentle eye contact when your partner speaks.
- It's using touch to comfort rather than to control.
- It's breathing before responding, so your energy says, "I'm here," even when emotions run high.

When our nonverbal signals align with love, they become a silent form of healing.

3. Spiritual Communication — Listening with the Heart

The third and deepest form of communication is spiritual. It transcends language and gestures. It is the exchange of energy, empathy, and intent. It's what happens when you *sense* what your partner feels before they say it, or when silence becomes sacred rather than awkward.

Spiritual communication is born of "**discernment**," the ability to perceive beyond words. It asks: *What is their soul really saying?* Sometimes a person's anger hides grief. Sometimes their silence conceals fear. Whole communicators don't rush to fix; they pause to feel. They pray before they speak and listen for divine guidance before they react.

In this way, spiritual communication mirrors God's own dialogue with us: gentle, patient, and rooted in love. It's not mystical; it's mindful. It's learning to recognize the divine imprint in another and responding from that awareness. When we listen spiritually, we stop hearing with our ears and start hearing with our hearts.

Whole communication integrates all three levels. Words (verbal) convey intention. Actions and tone (nonverbal) convey emotion. Presence and discernment (spiritual) convey truth. When all three are aligned, communication becomes an act of love, not just an exchange of information.

How to Listen for the Need Behind the Words

Listening is more than waiting for your turn to speak. It's the act of love that turns noise into understanding. Every word carries two messages: the one spoken and the one *felt.* Whole communication hears both.

Psychologist Sue Johnson teaches that behind every argument lies a *protest for connection*, a plea that sounds like criticism but is really fear in disguise (Johnson 2008). When someone says, "You never listen to me," they may truly be asking, *"Do I matter to you?"* When they say, "You're always busy," the hidden message may be, *"I miss you."* Whole communicators listen not only to what's being said but to what the soul is trying to express.

The Three Levels of Listening

1. **Surface Listening — Hearing Words:**
   This is where most communication stops. It takes in information but not meaning.
   Example: You hear, "I'm fine," and take it literally, though the tone says otherwise.
2. **Emotional Listening — Hearing Feelings:**
   This level tunes in to tone, expression, and energy. It notices that "I'm fine" really means, "I'm hurt, but I don't feel safe to say it."
3. **Soul Listening — Hearing Need:**
   This is the deepest level, where discernment meets empathy. It asks, *"What does this person's soul need right now: comfort, clarity, reassurance, or space?"*

Whole relationships depend on soul listening. They recognize that most conflict is not about *content* but about *connection.*

Listening Through the Lens of Soul Needs

Your earlier journey through the **Soul Needs framework** (universal and unique soul needs) now becomes practical.

- When you listen for truth, you seek understanding, not defense.
- When you listen for love, you stay present even when emotions run high.
- When you listen with faith, you trust that grace can repair what words have wounded.

This is what it means to listen whole. You aren't trying to win, fix, or explain; you're creating space for healing to occur.

Practices for Whole Listening

- **Pause** before responding. Silence can be sacred. Let your partner's words settle before forming your reply.
- **Reflect** what you hear. Say, "It sounds like you're feeling…" or "I hear that you need…" Reflection shows empathy without assumption.
- **Regulate** yourself first. You can't listen deeply when you're flooded with emotion. Breathe, pray, or pause to return to peace.
- **Ask** open questions. "Can you help me understand what you're needing right now?" turns conflict into collaboration.

When both people listen this way, communication stops being a transaction and becomes transformation.

Whole listening is the heartbeat of wholeness itself. It is where truth meets tenderness, where understanding replaces assumption, and where souls remember they are on the same side. Listening for the need behind the words is how love learns to heal without being asked.

Healthy communication is learned, not instinctive. If words tend to disappear under pressure, that is not a character flaw; it is a skill gap. The workbook offers practical language tools and reflection exercises to help you practice clear, respectful communication.

The Sacred Rhythm of Communication

Communication is the sacred rhythm of love, the continual exchange that keeps hearts in harmony. Whole communication is not about eloquence or persuasion; it's about presence. It invites us to speak truthfully, listen tenderly, and stay attuned to what words cannot say.

When we replace assumption with articulation, we invite clarity. When we align our words, tone, and spirit, we create safety. And when we listen for the need beneath the words, we turn conversation into communion.

> *"Every word carries two messages: the one spoken and the one felt."*

Wholeness in communication means choosing connection over control, understanding over ego, and grace over reaction. It's realizing that every dialogue is an opportunity to practice love in real time.

Communication reaches its highest form when it is wrapped in humility. To speak humbly is to honor another's soul as much as your own: to yield, forgive, and repair. The next chapter explores this quiet strength of love, where humility becomes not a lowering of self, but a lifting of both hearts toward wholeness.

16

HUMILITY: THE HIDDEN STRENGTH OF LOVE

Humility is the fuel that keeps the TORCH lit. It is the cornerstone of enduring love, the quiet posture that keeps hearts teachable and relationships whole. It reminds us that love is not about power, position, or pride, but about service. Surrender is expressed when both people choose respect over pride and understanding over control. This humility allows us to learn, to forgive, and to yield even when we are right.

To be humble, or to practice humility, means to value other people and their perspectives without indulging in pride. It is the opposite of boastfulness, arrogance, or vanity. Humility does not diminish confidence; it sanctifies it. It balances strength with softness and turns self-importance into self-awareness.

In the previous chapter, we explored how communication bridges gaps between hearts, but humility is what keeps that bridge standing. Without it, words become weapons and listening becomes a strategy rather than a service. Humility transforms dialogue into discovery. It teaches us to approach others not as opponents to be convinced, but as souls to be understood.

True humility is not weakness; it is wisdom. It recognizes that being "right" is rarely more important than being reconciled. It trades defensiveness for curiosity, accusation for compassion, and pride for peace.

Humility says, "*I can be firm in truth and still tender in tone.*" It says, "*I can disagree without dishonoring.*" It says, "*I can yield without losing myself.*"

When humility governs love, relationships stop competing and start collaborating. Each person becomes both teacher and student, learning from one another's humanity and growing in mutual grace.

The next sections explore how humility reveals itself through apology, forgiveness, and the servant's heart, the practices that make love strong enough to last and soft enough to heal.

Why Apology Is Power, and Forgiveness Is Fuel

Humility reveals its greatest strength in apology. Saying *"I'm sorry"* does not weaken love; it refines it. Apology is the moment pride surrenders to truth, when ego yields so that empathy can enter. It is how we acknowledge that our actions have caused harm and that the relationship matters more than our image.

Apology is not merely the confession of wrong; it is the declaration of value. It says, *"You matter enough for me to make this right."* In this way, apology becomes an act of love's highest intelligence, honoring both truth and tenderness at once.

Research supports this sacred truth. In *The Five Languages of Apology*, Gary Chapman and Jennifer Thomas (2006) identify five distinct ways people express remorse:

1. **Expressing regret** ("I'm sorry for how I hurt you.")
2. **Accepting responsibility** ("It was my fault; I was wrong.")
3. **Making restitution** ("How can I make this right?")
4. **Genuinely repenting** ("I want to change and not repeat this.")
5. **Requesting forgiveness** ("Will you forgive me?")

Whole relationships learn to speak all five languages. They understand that a simple "sorry" may open the door, but only consistent humility keeps it open.

Apology without accountability is empty; forgiveness without change is naïve. However, when humility powers both – when one admits fault and the other offers grace – the relationship becomes stronger than it was before the wound.

> *"An apology is power because it disarms pride. Forgiveness is fuel because it frees the heart to move forward."*

Forgiveness is not the denial of pain; it is the decision to stop carrying it. It does not excuse the offense, but it releases the offender and frees the heart from resentment. As Jesus taught, forgiveness is not seven times, but "seventy times seven," meaning without limit. Spiritually, this reflects God's own nature: always ready to restore and reconcile.

Forgiveness heals the forgiver as much as the forgiven. It breaks the invisible chains of resentment that choke love's potential. When we forgive, we return to peace; when we withhold forgiveness, we remain bound to the pain we refuse to release.

In a whole relationship, both apology and forgiveness flow from humility. Humility says, *"I am human enough to err and divine enough to restore."* It is the daily practice of remembering that reconciliation is greater than righteousness.

Learning to Yield Without Losing Yourself

To yield is not to give up; it is to give grace. Yielding in love means knowing when to soften, when to listen, and when to release control for the sake of peace. It's an act of strength wrapped in gentleness, the art of leading with empathy instead of ego.

Many fear that yielding means surrendering identity or betraying self-respect, but humility does not erase the self; it *expands* it. It allows you to see beyond the boundaries of your own perspective. To yield without losing yourself means staying grounded in truth while remaining open to transformation.

Yielding says, "*I can pause my pride to protect our peace.*" It says, "*I can listen fully before I defend.*" It says, "*I can choose love over control without abandoning myself.*"

In relationships, power struggles are almost always about fear: fear of losing influence, being misunderstood or appearing weak. Yet when both people practice humility, fear loses its grip. Each person learns to yield where love asks, trusting that the other will not take advantage of their openness.

From a psychological perspective, this is what researchers call *secure functioning*: both partners feeling safe enough to lower their defenses without losing their sense of self. It's an emotional dance that balances autonomy and connection: "*I can stand on my own two feet yet still stand beside you.*"

Spiritually, this mirrors Christ's example of surrender: strength under submission, authority expressed through love. Jesus washed the feet of those He led. That was not weakness; it was divine humility in motion. In the same way, humility in relationships doesn't reduce you. It *reveals* you.

To yield without losing yourself, remember these truths:

1. **Stay anchored in your values.** Yielding is not abandoning your convictions; it's expressing them with grace.
2. **Yield to truth, not to pressure.** Humility responds to what is right, not merely to what is requested.
3. **Discern timing.** Sometimes yielding means stepping back to listen; other times, it means speaking gently at the right moment.

Yielding is a sacred dance between confidence and compassion. When done from wholeness, it doesn't make you smaller, it makes love larger.

Healing Through Humility

Humility is not self-deprecation; it's self-reflection that opens the door to healing and wholeness. It is the quiet recognition that true strength begins with surrender, the willingness to see yourself honestly before demanding to be seen by another.

You have to be healed enough to properly handle what you're asking for: a *whole* relationship. Otherwise, you'll carry the same unhealed patterns into new connections and call the repetition "bad luck" or "bad partners." Meanwhile, humility whispers, *"Perhaps the pattern is not punishment, but invitation."* Humility says, *"Let me see myself clearly before I judge the mirror of another."* Yes, it's possible that someone mistreated or manipulated you. Perhaps you overfunctioned in your relationship, carrying emotional loads that were never yours to bear alone. Humility invites you to look deeper and ask, *"Why did I believe I had to?"*

The compulsion to fix, fill or feed every emotional void is not a sign of love; it is a sign of lack, an ache for approval disguised as devotion. That belief can exhaust you and alienate others. Healing doesn't mean becoming perfect; it means becoming *aware*. You gain awareness of how your wounds, expectations, and defenses shape your ability to love and be loved.

Humility gives us that awareness. It's the posture that turns pain into wisdom and self-protection into growth. Without humility, pride blinds us to the lessons hidden in our losses. Life will keep sending the same teacher until we become new students.

A new person may enter your life, but if your patterns remain unexamined, the story simply changes names. Unhealed places within us still speak. They trigger, distort, and project. Until we address the deeper source, we repeat the same story with new characters, wondering why the ending never changes.

That's why humility is the **ultimate act of surrender**. It bridges human brokenness and divine restoration. When we kneel before truth about ourselves, others, and God, we invite grace to do what pride cannot. Humility doesn't erase pain; it redeems it. It allows God to rebuild us from the inside out, transforming shame into strength and wounds into wisdom.

Pride resists healing because it fears exposure. Humility receives healing because it trusts grace. When we humble ourselves, we stop demanding that others complete us and start allowing God to *restore* us. Healing through humility is the sacred exchange of control for compassion, or of self-sufficiency for surrender. It is the moment we stop asking, *"Why me?"* and start asking, *"What is this trying to teach me?"*

Whole love cannot exist without this kind of surrender because humility is what makes reconciliation possible – with others and with ourselves.

A Servant's Heart

Wholeness begins within – a self-aware mind and a surrendered heart – but it cannot end there. Healing and humility prepare both mind and heart, yet love is proven in practice. The purpose of becoming whole is not about perfection, but about learning to love others from a place of freedom rather than fear.

From that freedom, humility takes root, and it naturally bears the fruit of **servanthood**. We no longer seek relationships to complete us; we enter them to contribute to others' growth. Love, at its highest form, becomes less about what we receive and more about what we are willing to give.

A servant's heart does not mean self-erasure; it means self-offering. It is the posture of love that sees another's need and responds with compassion, not control. Servanthood flows from spiritual maturity, the recognition that love's greatest expression is not domination but devotion.

Servanthood is humility in action, a love made tangible through care, patience, and sacrifice.

It asks not, *"What do I gain from this relationship?"* but *"How can I help this relationship flourish?"* It gives freely, without keeping score, because it understands that giving from wholeness never leads to depletion. It leads to divine replenishment.

This is what Christ modeled through every act of His ministry: the washing of feet, the feeding of the hungry, and the forgiveness of the unworthy. His humility was His power. His servanthood was His legacy. To love as He loved is to understand that service is a destiny, not a duty.

When we embody a servant's heart, relationships stop being arenas of performance and become places of purpose. We stop striving to be impressive and start striving to be impactful. We honor both our boundaries and our calling, knowing that love without service is sentiment, but love expressed through service becomes sacred.

As we transition into Part V, *The Practice of Whole Love*, we explore what this looks like in motion: how love unfolds in **phases**, deepens through **commitment**, and matures through **service**. This is where the wholeness we've cultivated within begins to extend outward, shaping how we show up, interact, and stay in relationships.

PART IV REVIEW: THE TORCH OF LOVE

Part IV introduced the TORCH — Trust, Openness, Respect, Communication, and Humility — the five expressions that illuminate how whole people love. You explored:

- what safe connection looks like,
- how vulnerability becomes revelation instead of risk,
- why respect sustains attraction,
- how communication builds bridges rather than walls,
- and how humility heals what pride destroys

In this regard, we learned that whole love is not performance; it is presence. It is the ability to show up with truth, empathy, reverence, and responsibility for the heart entrusted to you.

Whole love requires surrender of the ego. Each TORCH element reflects that courage to surrender:

Trust → surrender control
Openness → surrender protection
Respect → surrender superiority
Communication → surrender assumption
Humility → surrender pride

When connection is practiced with this kind of surrender, relationships move beyond attraction and compatibility. They begin to develop the stability required for commitment.

Loving others whole begins with loving yourself well, then expressing that inner truth through how you speak, listen, honor, and repair. When this posture of surrender becomes consistent, love matures into covenant.

When alignment becomes commitment, love moves from intention to endurance.

Before beginning Part V, review the affirmations in ***Appendix E*** *that support your healthy, whole connection to others and the journal prompts in* ***Appendix F*** *that likewise complement this aim.*

PART V

THE PRACTICE OF WHOLE LOVE

From Alignment to Covenant

17

PHASES OF LOVE

Most adults have experienced both love and heartbreak, but I've learned that the worst pain isn't losing someone you love. It's realizing you're in love with someone you don't actually like or respect. That kind of love leaves you questioning your own judgment.

After my divorce, I made a vow: I would only be with a man who could also be my best friend and I, his. I would never again allow charisma to replace core values or focus on potential and ignore patterns. Friendship became my new foundation for love. A partner who cannot also be a friend will eventually feel like a stranger. Friendship allows love to mature beyond attraction into companionship, trust, and respect.

My goal in love has been simple: to see if I *like* a person as much as I may feel love for him. Liking someone takes time, shared experiences, and honesty. You never want to rush ahead and commit to someone you later realize you don't respect or even enjoy.

Let's face it, relationships revolve around love, finding it, maintaining it, and sharing it. Everyone wants to be loved, but few take the time to truly understand what love is. Most people confuse true love with the phases that come before it, mistaking temporary feelings for lasting truth. That confusion is why we often give too much too soon or hold back when the moment calls for more.

To love wisely, we have to recognize where we are emotionally. Love unfolds in phases, each revealing a different part of our hearts. When we name these feelings honestly, we protect ourselves from mistaking emotion for intention.

Understanding What You Feel Before You Call It Love

Many people fall in love too soon, not necessarily with a person, but with the *feeling* of possibility. We sense connection and assume meaning. We project intention where there is only curiosity. That's why emotional awareness is essential: it helps us name what we're feeling so we don't hand our hearts over to an illusion.

Love grows through stages, but these stages are *feelings*, not commitments. Each phase reveals something about our inner state – how ready, secure, or self-aware we are – and invites us to pause before we assume the other person feels the same.

1. Attraction — "I feel drawn to you."

Attraction is the first spark. It might be physical, intellectual, energetic or spiritual magnetic pull toward another person. It's exciting and full of potential, but it tells us nothing yet about compatibility or purpose.

Wholeness check: Enjoy the feeling without calling it destiny. Observe before you interpret.
Common misunderstanding: Believing chemistry equals connection or divine confirmation
How heartbreak happens: Assuming mutual appeal when attraction is one-sided

2. Interest — "I want to know more."

Interest moves beyond the spark into curiosity. We start asking questions, spending time, and discovering who the other person is beneath the surface.

Wholeness check: Let curiosity guide you, not fantasy. Notice what's real.
Common misunderstanding: Confusing *eligibility* (they look good on paper) with *interest* (they're genuinely enthralled)
How heartbreak happens: Mistaking polite attention for pursuit or interpreting your effort as mutual interest

3. Like — "I enjoy you."

Liking is that comfortable resonance when you simply enjoy someone's presence. You may laugh easily, share stories, and feel emotionally at ease.

Wholeness check: Determine whether the connection is positive or enjoyable.

Common misunderstanding: Assuming emotional comfort means emotional commitment.

How heartbreak happens: One person invests in the bond while the other only enjoys the moment.

4. Admiration — "I value you."

Admiration involves appreciation of personality and/or character. This means having appreciation for who the person *is*, not just how they make you feel.

Wholeness check: Be sure you respect them before you claim to *love* them.

Common misunderstanding: Falling "in love" before you've confirmed you actually like the person behind the feeling

How heartbreak happens: Being enamored with the idea of someone rather than their reality

5. Love — "I choose to care, grow, and give."

Love is more than emotion; it's the blending of feeling and choice. Real love transcends chemistry and preference. It honors truth, accepts imperfection, and seeks growth for both people.

Wholeness check: Ask, *Is my love freeing or fearful?* Real love frees; attachment clings.

Common misunderstanding: Mistaking need, control, or dependency for devotion

How heartbreak happens: Loving without boundaries or without mutual commitment

Each phase of love answers a different question about the relationship. Attraction asks, *Am I drawn to you?* Interest asks, *Do I want to know you?* Liking asks, *Do I enjoy being with you?* Admiration asks, *Do I value who you are?* Love ultimately asks, *Can we build a life aligned in truth together?* Skipping phases means skipping crucial, incremental questions.

Each phase of love reveals something different about the relationship. When we move too quickly, we skip the discernment each phase provides.

Phase	What it Discerns
Attraction	chemistry
Interest	curiosity
Like	emotional comfort
Admiration	character
Love	alignment and commitment

Hope, The Wild Card

Hope is an *emotional undercurrent* that can appear at any point. It's the dream of what *could be.* Hope keeps us open to love, but when it runs ahead of reality, it becomes fantasy.

Wholeness check: Hope wisely, not blindly. Look for evidence of shared intention.

Common misunderstanding: Building expectations before there is agreement

How heartbreak happens: Living in potential instead of truth, loving the idea of a relationship more than the person in it

The Confusion: When Feelings Outrun Facts

Attraction can feel like destiny. Affinity can feel like permanence. Hope can feel like commitment. However, feelings are *signals*, not *certificates.* They invite exploration, not assumption. When we move too fast, assigning meaning, titles or future plans before mutual intention is confirmed, we set ourselves up for heartbreak born of misunderstanding, not betrayal. Hope typically fuels these assumptions perhaps because of what we believe the other person is thinking or doing.

Hope without confirmation or clear *intention* is what keeps us in "situationships." Intention is a *decision* that can appear at any point but must be *mutual* to move love forward. It's what transforms connection into relationship. Without shared intention, there's only assumption.

One of the greatest challenges in love is confusing *intention* with any one of its phases. This is how many of us slip into or remain stuck in what we now call "situationships." We feel something real – a connection, an energy, a vibe – and assume it means the same thing to the other person.

Connection simply means there is mutual allure or resonance; it does not mean there is mutual *intention.* Intention requires a conscious choice to see, select, and pursue another person as a partner. When we mistake attraction for intention, affection for interest or hope for alignment, we start building emotional castles in the sand that easily get washed away with the tide of truth. We make plans, spend money, open our hearts, and even shape our futures around a connection that was never clearly defined.

Misunderstanding at any phase of love can cause deep heartbreak. Attraction mistaken for commitment leaves us disillusioned. Involvement without alignment breeds resentment. Hope without honesty births despair. To love wisely, we must learn to name what phase we're in and confirm that both hearts are in the same place before we give what can't easily be taken back.

Ultimately, love may be sparked by feeling, but it endures by choice, the daily commitment to respect, honor, support, serve, and trust. Whole love requires whole awareness: to ask, What am I truly feeling, and what is actually being reciprocated? This emotional honesty protects us from building futures on fantasy and calling wishful thinking "God's will." Love cannot make us whole if we keep outsourcing discernment to desire. This is how we stay present, not premature.

Emotional Maturity: Where Love Meets Alignment

Emotional maturity is what transforms love from an emotional experience into an intentional relationship. It's the ability to love with both the *heart* and the *mind*, to feel deeply while also thinking clearly. Without maturity, love is easily hijacked by fantasy. With it, love can grow into something steady, safe, and enduring.

One of the greatest tests of emotional maturity is **alignment**, the degree to which two people share similar values, vision, and direction. Feelings may bring two hearts together, but alignment determines whether they can *walk together.* Scripture asks, *"Can two walk together unless they be agreed?"* That question still holds the wisdom to keep us from unnecessary heartbreak.

Maturity in love is revealed through stewardship of both emotion and responsibility. If you cannot manage your emotions or your money, you are not yet ready for a committed relationship. Both are forms of stewardship that reveal your capacity for self-control, discipline, and trustworthiness. Emotional maturity means you can respond rather than react, communicate rather than criticize, and take responsibility rather than assign blame. Financial maturity shows that you value planning, accountability, and delayed gratification – all essential in building a stable union. The inability to manage either will eventually fracture the foundation of trust in any relationship.

Alignment in Practice

Alignment doesn't mean sameness; it means harmony. You don't have to think, vote, worship, or dream identically, but you must be able to honor and build with one another in truth. Alignment shows up in how two people approach purpose, family, faith, finances, time, and even conflict. In practice, it can be understood in three ways:

- **Healthy:** We have honest conversations about goals, beliefs, and lifestyle. Mature love faces reality, not fantasy.
- **Misunderstood:** We avoid hard truths because they threaten the comfort of connection. One or both people may have to shrink or deny soul needs.
- **Ignored:** When we ignore misalignment, we enter situations built on illusion instead of truth. This leads to potential heartbreak.

When emotional maturity is lacking, we start explaining away red flags instead of examining them. We rationalize incompatibility with phrases like, *"Every relationship takes work,"* or *"We'll grow into it."* However, growth without agreement is strain, not progress. Love can only mature when both people are moving in the same spiritual and emotional direction.

Emotional Maturity as Wholeness

To love maturely is to love *whole.* Whole love doesn't cling out of fear or shrink out of pride. It communicates openly, listens humbly, and seeks peace over ego. Maturity understands that feelings may fade or fluctuate, but truth endures. The emotionally mature person asks, *"Are we aligned in purpose, not just attracted in emotion?"*

Emotional maturity demands courage, the courage to see clearly, speak honestly, and walk away peacefully when alignment isn't there. That courage protects the heart from building castles on sand.

> *"Love may begin with connection, but it matures through alignment. Without shared truth, even the strongest attraction will eventually unravel."*

Bridge to Wholeness: The Courage to Face Your Truth

Emotional maturity isn't just about choosing the right partner; it's about becoming the kind of person who can handle truth, even when it's uncomfortable. Love without truth becomes fantasy; truth without love becomes cruelty. Wholeness requires both. It takes courage to admit when something or someone no longer aligns with your purpose, and even more courage to stay when growth demands patience instead of escape.

When you're whole, you stop needing relationships to validate your worth. You seek alignment, not attachment; honesty, not illusion. You recognize that love cannot make you whole if you're unwilling to face the parts of yourself that resist truth. That is the real work of love: the courage to grow, to let go, or to remain, all in the name of becoming fully yourself.

Truth is one of our core universal soul needs. It anchors love and gives faith its direction. Love awakens the heart; faith keeps it open; but truth keeps it honest. Without truth, love loses integrity, and faith drifts into fantasy. Together, love, faith, and truth create the inner balance that allows relationships to grow without losing the self.

To live and love whole is to let truth establish love, and to let faith sustain it, trusting that what aligns with your soul will never require you to abandon it.

If you feel tempted to rush toward certainty, pause here. Sometimes clarity comes not from deciding quickly, but from listening more slowly. Journal your thoughts or feelings that may have emerged while reading.

18

COMMITTING TO OTHERS

In whole relationships, committing to others involves **surrender and servanthood**. This means actively seeking the best for the other person while understanding that your efforts may not always be reciprocated in the same way or at the same time. This giving of oneself requires trust, respect, and humility.

Don't commit to someone unless you're ready to give, not just receive. True love requires servanthood, not self-service. A whole relationship calls for two people who see commitment not as a **comfort zone** but as a **contribution zone** where each person gives of themselves to uplift, support, and help the other grow. Love matures when sacrifice replaces selfishness. If your primary question is *"What will I get from this?"* instead of *"What can I give to this?"* then you are not ready for commitment.

At its root, commitment means to *entrust* or *pledge oneself* to a cause, person, or covenant. In the biblical sense, it is an act of stewardship, honoring the sacred responsibility of another's heart. When we commit, we agree to be accountable for our words, our presence, and our impact. Commitment is not a contract of convenience; it's a covenant of character.

Too often, people confuse **connection** with **commitment.** Connection is emotional. Commitment is intentional. Connection happens by feeling; commitment happens by decision. Feelings can fluctuate, but a covenant decision anchors love through every season.

In today's culture, commitment is often misrepresented as *loss of freedom.* In truth, commitment is the highest form of freedom, the freedom to love consistently without fear, distraction, or divided loyalty. It releases you from the chaos of indecision and the instability of emotional impulse. When two whole people commit, they are not binding themselves in restriction; they are joining themselves in purpose. True commitment doesn't demand perfection; it demands **presence.** It is the steady "yes" that echoes even when emotions say "no."

Premature Commitments

Premature commitment happens when we attach before understanding, invest before alignment, or promise before purpose. It's the pattern of giving long-term energy to short-term chemistry. Each phase of love has its own function, but when we skip steps, rushing from attraction to attachment, we end up emotionally over-invested in relationships that were never meant to carry that weight.

The Lure of Attraction

Every romantic story begins with attraction. It's what draws us into connection. Attraction can come from beauty, charisma, intelligence, humor, or even shared pain. However, attraction alone is not evidence of compatibility.

The caution is that many confuse **attraction** with **love** or even **like.** Attraction is a spark that is sometimes thrilling and sometimes overwhelming, but it cannot sustain a flame on its own. It is *reactive*, not *reflective.*

Research from behavioral psychologist Charles Chu (2023) supports this, showing that we're often drawn to people we believe share our inner essence or worldview. In a series of studies, Chu and researcher Brian Lowery found that individuals who believe they possess a deep inner essence – what psychologists call "*self-essentialist reasoning*" – tend to assume that others who share even one common interest also share their broader worldview. Yet this perception can be deceiving; one shared interest doesn't guarantee long-term alignment.

When we try to commit during the attraction phase, we mistake emotional intensity for relational depth. Attraction may start the story, but only compatibility, friendship, and shared purpose can keep it unfolding.

> *"Attraction is the spark that lights connection,*
> *but it can't keep the fire burning."*

When Interest Is Not Mutual

Interest often follows attraction. Once someone captures our attention, curiosity grows. We want to know more about them, spend time around them, and explore the possibility of connection.

However, strong attraction can sometimes distort discernment. When we feel drawn to someone, we may pursue them so eagerly that we forget to ask an essential question: **Are they equally interested in us?**

Interest must be mutual to move forward in a healthy direction. Without reciprocity, curiosity becomes pursuit rather than connection.

Sometimes people continue expressing interest even when the other person has shown little genuine investment. This can happen in **direct** ways, such as initiating conversation, making plans, or revealing personal feelings, or in **indirect** ways, such as lingering attention, subtle compliments, or repeated attempts to remain close. Personality, past experiences, and unresolved wounds can influence how openly someone expresses their interest.

Yet interest that is not reciprocated cannot mature into a healthy, whole relationship. Instead, it often leads to imbalance.

In some cases, the other person may enjoy the attention without offering true commitment. They respond just enough to keep the connection alive – an occasional message, a vague promise, a small gesture – while never fully investing. This pattern, often called "breadcrumbing," can create the illusion of progress while the relationship remains emotionally one-sided.

This is where self-respect and self-confidence become essential. When you value yourself, you recognize that mutual interest is the minimum requirement for moving forward. A whole relationship cannot develop when one person is pursuing while the other is merely receiving.

Interest is meant to reveal curiosity on both sides. When curiosity flows in only one direction, the phase has already answered its question. Interest opens the door to discovery, but only mutual interest allows a relationship to grow.

The Power of Like

Philosopher Friedrich Nietzsche observed, *"It is not a lack of love, but a lack of friendship that makes unhappy marriages."* Liking someone may be quieter than loving them, but it's more enduring.

Love is often emotional intensity; liking is emotional ease. To like someone means to enjoy who they are, including their personality, humor, habits or rhythm of life. Conversation feels natural. Time together feels comfortable rather than draining. You are not constantly managing tension or performing for approval.

This stage reveals something critical about relational compatibility: **Can we enjoy life together?**

You can admire someone's achievements, feel attracted to their appearance, and even care deeply about their well-being, yet still discover that you do not actually enjoy their company. When liking is absent, relationships often feel heavy and effortful. Affection becomes obligation, and admiration slowly turns into endurance.

Liking forms the friendship foundation that sustains love once passion cools. Attraction may ignite the relationship, and admiration may elevate it, but friendship stabilizes it. When the butterflies fade and life becomes ordinary again, friendship remains the bridge that keeps hearts connected.

In many ways, liking is where relational peace is first tested. If two people cannot enjoy each other in ordinary moments, long-term harmony becomes difficult to sustain. Attraction may spark a relationship, but liking determines whether it can live.

Admiration Can Be Misleading

Admiration is often mistaken for love because it carries genuine respect. When we admire someone, we recognize qualities we value, such as their character, competence, skill, discipline, kindness, or strength. We appreciate who they appear to be, and that appreciation can create a powerful pull toward connection.

Research by John Gottman highlights how important admiration is in healthy relationships. In "*The Seven Principles for Making Marriage Work*," he explains that fondness and admiration form a crucial emotional foundation for lasting couples. Even when partners frustrate one another, they continue to see each other as worthy of honor and respect (Gottman and Silver 2015). In this sense, admiration acts as an antidote to contempt.

Respect is such a powerful relational resource that it can sustain a connection even when romantic emotion is limited. This may help explain why some arranged marriages succeed. Though love may not begin as the driving force, mutual respect provides stability and dignity within the relationship.

However, admiration can also be deceptive when it appears before deeper compatibility is known. It is possible to admire someone greatly and still not enjoy them as a partner. A person may be talented, respected, intelligent, or highly responsible – all qualities worthy of admiration – yet share little common ground with you in personality, lifestyle, or values.

This is why the phases of love should not be rushed or skipped. Admiration may convince you that someone is an excellent person, but love requires more than recognizing excellence. It requires compatibility, shared values, and a genuine sense of connection.

For example, you may admire a coworker's discipline, intelligence, or leadership. You may even feel attracted to their competence and drive. Yet you may not enjoy their personality or personal choices (dislike them). In the same way, someone might marry a person admired for beauty, success, or reputation and later discover that admiration cannot replace genuine connection. Essentially, admiration alone does not guarantee emotional compatibility or relational harmony.

Admiration is an important stage of relational discovery, but it is not the destination. When admiration matures through the earlier phases (attraction, interest, and liking) it can contribute to lasting love. When it appears in isolation, however, it can create the illusion of compatibility where none truly exists. Ultimately, admiration recognizes excellence, but love requires alignment.

Codependency as Hope

Sometimes premature commitment hides behind something that *feels noble*: hope. Codependency often masquerades as hopefulness, believing that if we love hard enough, wait long enough, or sacrifice enough, the other person will become who we know they can be.

However, hope based on potential rather than reality leads to self-neglect. When affection is inconsistent, those brief moments of warmth feel like proof that change is coming. The cycle becomes addictive: distance, pursuit, reconciliation, repeat.

Caretaking then replaces connection. You manage their moods, ignore your own needs, and call it love. In truth, it's fear disguised as loyalty. The fear of letting go sounds like faith: *"If I leave, I'll miss the moment they finally change."* However, that isn't faith in God; it's misplaced faith in control.

Ask yourself:

- Are my hopes grounded in consistent action or isolated moments?
- Am I loving who they are now or who I wish they'd become?

If the answer leans toward potential, it's projection, not partnership.

> *"Codependency looks like loyalty, but it's really fear wearing hope's clothing."*

Attachment vs. Love

One of the clearest signs of premature commitment is attachment mistaken for love. Attachment clings; love frees. Attachment says, *"I love you because you make me feel whole."* Genuine love says, *"I love you because I already am whole."*

Attachment seeks to possess, protect, and preserve the source of comfort. Love seeks to bless, honor, and empower the beloved. When our sense of worth depends on someone else's presence, we are attached, not in love.

Attachment is born of fear, including fear of loss, fear of loneliness, fear of not being enough. Love, by contrast, is rooted in peace. It wants what's best for the other person, even if that means letting them choose a path apart from us.

> *"Attachment says, 'Don't leave me.' Love says, 'I want you to be free.'"*

Committing Everything

True commitment requires more than emotion; it requires integration of the whole self. It is holistic and involves every part of our being:

- **Emotional:** sharing authentic feelings.
- **Mental:** aligning thoughts, goals, and communication.
- **Physical:** honoring health, affection, and respect for one another's bodies.
- **Social:** integrating lives, families, and communities.
- **Spiritual:** sharing values, purpose, and vision.

Partial commitment, where someone gives emotionally but not mentally, or physically but not spiritually, creates imbalance. It's why some couples can live together but still feel worlds apart.

Fear of rejection or failure often causes people to withhold full commitment. Yet wholeness invites us to give completely, not recklessly but consciously. A whole person isn't afraid to commit because they know the relationship does not define them; it *refines* them.

> *"Whole love is never partial. It gives freely because it knows it can stand alone."*

When we skip phases – mistaking attraction for affection, liking for love, or attachment for covenant – we often wake up in **broken love:** a relationship where we've over-committed before clarity or readiness. The next sections explore how those premature commitments evolve into emotional imbalance and how to heal when they break.

If you are feeling stirred, heavy, or emotionally exposed, this is a good place to stop reading for now. Recognition can open old wounds before healing begins, and that does not mean you are doing this wrong.

Broken Love: When Commitment Hurts More Than It Heals

Not every relationship that looks committed is healthy. Some commitments are formed out of fear, obligation or emotional deficit. These are what I call **broken loves**, which are relationships between people who are unhealed or broken, operating from wounds rather than wisdom. These patterns are often described as "*trauma bonds*," but I call them *broken loves.* They are commitments formed from *woundedness*, not wholeness, and from *emotional survival*, not divine order.

Commitment moves a relationship forward in an intentional, definitive way, making both people feel more secure. This, of course, happens in marriage, but even in dating, commitment creates a sense of belonging and safety. When this commitment happens too early, especially during the *attraction* or *like* phase, it can be confusing. If one person is doing all the giving, the relationship becomes one-sided. This imbalance is a sign of broken love.

Broken love occurs when one or both individuals enter a commitment carrying unhealed trauma or unmet emotional needs. These wounds distort how we connect, communicate, and interpret love. As explored in Chapter 2, brokenness creates patterns, but when two broken people bond, those patterns often collide rather than complement.

In these relationships, an unhealed partner often wreaks havoc, either consciously or unconsciously, sabotaging the relationship as a defense mechanism. It's self-protection gone awry. Perhaps they learned early on that expecting good things often led to disappointment, criticism or rejection. So, to avoid that potential pain, they reject the relationship before it can reject them. This preemptive strategy keeps them from feeling too hopeful or too deserving. It's as if their mind says:

"If I don't let myself get too happy, it won't hurt as much when it's taken away."

That mindset, though protective, quietly poisons intimacy. When you expect loss, you unconsciously prepare for it, and sometimes even provoke it.

They may also experience a loss of compassion, both toward themselves and others. When love from caregivers was tied to performance or perfection, they never learned that compassion could exist simply because they existed. So now, when they make a mistake or feel insecure, they instinctively criticize themselves before anyone else can. It's another form of preemptive rejection, a way to stay in control of their own pain. Thus, broken people break their committed relationships.

Mixed Signals

In broken love, *mixed signals* are often the norm. You may experience warmth and affection one moment, cold detachment the next. That intermittent reinforcement becomes addictive, like chasing something always just out of reach.

When you're prone to interpreting love through a lens of rejection, even small gestures of attention can carry enormous weight. It creates a **push-pull broken love cycle** that looks like this:

- You pursue or initiate communication to feel close.
- They withdraw or breadcrumb, offering just enough to keep you engaged.
- You suppress your needs to maintain the connection.
- The cycle repeats.

Each round deepens the emotional dependency and reinforces the false hope that things might change if only you try harder, give more, or wait longer.

Optimistic to a Fault

Some people stay in broken love not because they're weak, but because they're *hopeful*. You may assume others are fundamentally good and capable of growth, making it difficult to walk away. You believe in potential, and that belief can keep you bound to people who are unwilling or unable to reciprocate.

You may also have learned that compromising your needs is the *price of love.* Perhaps a part of you believes your needs aren't as important as theirs, a belief inherited from childhood, not truth. Healthy relationships don't require self-erasure to keep them going. Love cannot be sustained by one person's optimism and the other's avoidance.

Emotionally Unavailable

Being in a relationship with someone who is emotionally unavailable can be especially painful. The question *"Where do we stand?"* rarely gets answered directly, leaving you confused and depleted. So, why would anyone stay in a broken relationship with someone who is emotionally unavailable and resists commitment? In short, they stay because of *the hope of connection*, especially when love feels conditional or uncertain. This can be more compelling than the reality of disconnection. For someone whose early attachments taught them that love must be *earned*, even inconsistent affection feels like progress. It's a heartbreaking illusion: what feels familiar begins to feel safe, even when it isn't.

Seeking Validation

Many people stay in broken love because it offers temporary validation, the illusion of being chosen, remembered or still wanted. Similarly, when someone who has caused confusion or pain reappears, it can momentarily soothe the ache of rejection. Thoughts like, *"Maybe he still cares"* or *"I must have mattered after all"* can feel reassuring, but that reassurance is often short-lived. Real validation looks like:

- Someone showing up consistently, not when they sense you're slipping away.
- Someone who's clear about how they feel and brave enough to communicate it.
- Someone who makes you feel safe, not just "wanted."

If someone's return or apology doesn't come with changed behavior or emotional safety, it's just a flash of attention that quiets old insecurities before reigniting them. True validation isn't found in someone's return or willingness to stay in a broken relationship; it's revealed in their consistency and commitment to wholeness. It's the kind of love that shows up without needing to be chased, clarified or convinced.

Wanting to Feel Safe

Others remain in broken love because it feels familiar, not because it feels right. The search for safety outside oneself often begins in childhood, where love may have been unpredictable or conditional. That early instability teaches the nervous system to equate vigilance with security. As adults, this translates into scanning relationships for signs of rejection, betrayal or withdrawal.

Again, this is usually due to inconsistent caregiving in childhood or even past relationships in which your partner was unfaithful or chose someone else. If love consistently felt unstable, you learned:

- "I need to stay alert so I'm not blindsided."
- "I can't fully relax into love because it could be taken away."
- "If I find the problem first, I can avoid the pain later."

No partner can create lasting safety for someone who doesn't yet believe they are safe within themselves. When peace feels foreign, chaos can seem like home. Real safety begins when you stop outsourcing your sense of worth to another person and start anchoring it in truth, faith, and wholeness.

When Love Carries More Than It Can Hold

Avoidance and over-functioning are different strategies rooted in the same need for safety. When left unexamined, these patterns often harden into behaviors that place unbearable weight on love itself.

In some relationships, avoidance evolves into emotional numbing or addiction, where substances or compulsions replace presence. Addiction often emerges when avoidance becomes chemically outsourced. In others, fear expresses itself as control or abuse, where power is used as a substitute for vulnerability. Abuse reflects over-functioning for power rather than care. Still others fracture through infidelity, where distance is maintained through secrecy instead of honesty. Infidelity is avoidance disguised as desire.

These are not isolated issues, but patterns that have hardened over time which place demands on love that love alone cannot hold. They are often the downstream effects of protection strategies that once made sense but were never designed to sustain intimacy.

Love does not fail in these relationships because it is absent. It fails because it is asked to carry what only wholeness can hold — accountability, safety, responsibility, and truth.

Understanding this or them does not excuse harm, nor does it minimize the seriousness of these outcomes. It simply clarifies why love alone, no matter how sincere, cannot heal what was never examined.

If this section brings up memories of commitment that harmed rather than healed, pause here. This reflection belongs in your journal, where there is room for grief and truth without pressure.

Trauma: The Roots of Broken Love

Because my mother blatantly showed favoritism among her children, my early conditioning taught me that love meant self-abandonment. I had learned that being myself wasn't "enough" to earn attention or affection, and I needed to be more like my other siblings, her favorites, to gain approval. That favoritism silently instilled the belief that I had to *try harder, give more or shrink* to be chosen.

Many broken relationships trace back to early experiences of criticism, judgment, or conditional love. When a child grows up being shamed or ignored by people who were supposed to love them unconditionally, it shapes how they see themselves and what they believe they deserve.

When a child is repeatedly disparaged, blamed, or made to feel "not enough," they internalize those messages. Over time, this becomes a deep, subconscious belief:

- "I'm not good enough."
- "Something is wrong with me."
- "I don't deserve love unless I'm perfect or useful."

Even as an adult, you may *know* you deserve love, but the emotional part of you shaped by years of conditional acceptance still operates on outdated wiring.

Familiar pain often feels safer than unfamiliar peace. So, when love, stability, or success arrive, that old part of you feels *unsafe.* It may try to "correct" the imbalance by self-sabotaging, criticizing yourself, or choosing partners who recreate the emotional chaos you once survived.

When love was selective or scarce growing up, you learned to overextend yourself to keep it. You may have been the peacemaker, the achiever or the giver. Later in life, those same strategies resurface:

"If I can just prove I'm worthy, they'll finally love me."

It isn't conscious. It's *patterned.* Recognizing these origins doesn't condemn you, but rather it empowers you. Because once you identify the source of your broken love, you can begin to heal the parts of you that confuse attention for love, struggle for intimacy, or endurance for worth.

> *"Familiar pain often feels safer than unfamiliar peace, but peace is what wholeness requires."*

Healing from Misplaced Commitment

Healing begins the moment you recognize that the pattern isn't serving your wholeness. Awareness itself is the first act of restoration. As *Whole Relationships* teaches, wholeness begins with **self-awareness**, seeing yourself clearly in the mirror of your experiences. The fact that you can name what's broken means you've already stepped out of the cycle. That's power.

1. How Healing Starts

Experiencing broken love can be devastating because we often swing between self-blame and blame of the other person. Both extremes prevent us from looking into the *soul mirror* at what we allowed, ignored, or repeated. Healing asks for curiosity instead of condemnation.

If your partner is willing to work on their wounds, reconciliation is possible. Whether or not the relationship continues, the internal wiring can be changed. It may not be your fault or theirs, but it *is* within your power to shift it.

2. Re-Parenting and Relational Healing

Much of what we call "relationship conflict" is really *childhood pain seeking resolution.* When we haven't learned to re-parent ourselves — to comfort, affirm, and set boundaries within — we subconsciously look for partners to do it for us. We begin expecting others to fill the role of the nurturing parent we never had, or to silence the critical voice we still carry. However, that burden is too heavy for any partner to bear.

Re-parenting is what frees us to love without projection or dependency. When you learn to soothe your own fear of abandonment, you stop demanding constant reassurance. When you can affirm your own worth, you no longer need validation to feel secure. And when you can protect your peace, you stop mistaking control for care.

Healthy commitment begins when two people who have learned to re-parent themselves meet, not to fix each other, but to *fellowship* in wholeness.

3. The Shift: Cultivating Internal Safety

Healing doesn't mean becoming hyper-independent or detached. It means building enough inner ground so you don't feel like you're in freefall when someone pulls back or disappoints you.

Here's what cultivating inner safety can look like:

- **Self-reassurance:** "I can hold myself right now. I've been through worse."
- **Recognizing emotional flashbacks:** noticing when fear belongs to the past, not the present.
- **Re-wiring your response to quiet love:** stable love may feel unfamiliar, but it's secure.
- **Building body-based safety:** grounding, breathwork, or somatic therapy help your nervous system believe what your mind knows.
- **Creating boundaries that affirm:** "I don't need to abandon myself to stay close to someone."

We are not called to *chase* safety in others. We are called to *build* it within. Choose partners who meet you there, not as saviors, but as companions.

4. From Co-dependence to Independence

Breaking free from a codependent dynamic is one of the most self-honoring decisions you can make. Below is a guide that moves you from emotional entanglement to empowered clarity.

Step 1: Get Clear on Reality, Not Potential

What to do:
Create two columns: "Who they are now" vs. "Who I imagine they could become."
Why it helps:
Hope can blur reality. Clarity restores truth, and truth is the antidote to illusion.

Step 2: Reconnect with Your Soul Needs and Boundaries

What to do:
List what you need to feel secure and valued, your non-negotiables.
Why it helps:
This shifts the question from *"How do I keep them?"* to *"What honors me?"*

Step 3: Sit with Discomfort Without Fixing It

What to do:
Pause before reacting to mixed signals. Name the feeling: "This is anxiety, not intuition."
Why it helps:
Tolerating discomfort builds resilience and ends the reflex to chase reassurance.

Step 4: Seek Safe Support

What to do:
Engage therapy, recovery groups (like CoDA), or trusted friends who speak truth.
Why it helps:
Healing in isolation is hard. Support mirrors your growth when you can't yet see it.

Step 5: Redefine What Love Means

Reflect on:
Do you equate love with sacrifice, chaos, or waiting?
Rewrite your definition:
Love is calm, reciprocal, consistent, being chosen freely and respected without performance.

Step 6: Release the Outcome

What to do:
Stop bargaining your peace for someone else's potential.
Say: *"Even if they never change, I still deserve connection that honors me now."*
Why it helps:
Letting go of the outcome creates freedom; it ends the habit of self-abandonment in the name of hope.

> *"Healing begins when you stop focusing on others and start restoring yourself."*

5. Releasing Without Closing Your Heart

Letting go of an unhealthy, broken love attachment is not the same as shutting down your capacity to love. In fact, releasing someone from your grip or vice versa is often what restores your heart's natural rhythm. Holding on out of fear only keeps you connected to pain; releasing from love sets both hearts free.

When we let go in wholeness, we are not rejecting the person; we are releasing the pattern. We are saying, *"I honor what this taught me, but I will no longer let it define me."* That's not coldness; that's courage.

Letting go without closing your heart requires three inner shifts:

1. **Forgiveness over bitterness.**
   Forgiveness doesn't excuse what happened; it releases you from replaying it. Bitterness binds you to the moment of betrayal, while forgiveness reclaims your peace.
2. **Acceptance over avoidance.**
   You don't have to rewrite history to move on. You only have to accept what it was and what it was not. Acceptance brings truth to the surface, and truth always sets you free.
3. **Compassion over control.**
   Compassion allows you to say, "I understand why I stayed," without shame. Control says, "I'll never let this happen again," but compassion says, "I've learned enough to choose differently next time."

When we release with love, we make space for divine replacement. What was draining is replaced by what is destined. Love doesn't stop when we walk away; it simply evolves into peace.

> *"Release doesn't close your heart; it clears the space for God to fill it."*

6. Restoring Trust After Commitment Trauma

Commitment trauma is what happens when the people or promises we trusted most became the sources of our deepest pain. Betrayal, inconsistency, and abandonment can condition the heart to see love as dangerous and trust as weakness. However, as the TORCH reminds us, *trust* and *openness* are essential elements of whole love. Without them, intimacy becomes impossible, and even healthy relationships feel threatening.

This is why healing doesn't end with forgiveness; it continues with *retraining trust.* You must show your heart that safety can coexist with intimacy again. When trust has been violated, your instinct is to protect yourself through distance, control, or perfectionism. Healing trust means learning discernment, not building walls.

Start by noticing where fear of repetition is running the show. Ask yourself, *"Am I protecting my peace, or am I avoiding my potential?"* Learning to trust again is not about blind vulnerability; it's about *wise openness.*

Healing means rebuilding trust wisely – first with God, then with yourself, and finally with others. It's a process of relearning safety through the wisdom of discernment. When we practice this prudent openness after pain, we're not exposing ourselves recklessly. We're exercising faith that love can still be good.

When trust is rebuilt on truth instead of trauma or fantasy, you stop choosing people who trigger your wounds and start attracting those who reflect your wholeness.

> *"Trust and openness are not risks; they are the rewards of healing."*

As you move into the latter part of this chapter, this may be an appropriate moment to pause and simply reflect on the impact of what you've just discerned about healing in wholeness.

Re-defining Commitment in Wholeness

When two whole people come together, commitment looks and feels different. It's no longer a desperate attempt to secure love or prove worth; it becomes a conscious, covenantal choice rooted in freedom, not fear.

Wholeness doesn't promise perfection; it promises presence. Mature commitment means showing up consistently, communicating honestly, and choosing love daily even when feelings fluctuate. Whole partners understand that commitment isn't a one-time declaration; it's a rhythm of renewal, continually choosing one another in faith, respect, and grace.

What Mature Commitment Looks Like

A mature commitment is *mutual*, not mechanical. It's fueled by understanding, not obligation. When both people are whole, they come together not to complete each other, but to **complement** each other.

Whole partners bring self-awareness into the relationship. They recognize their triggers without projecting them, communicate needs without manipulation, and take responsibility for their peace. In this kind of love, both people can be vulnerable without losing identity, and accountable without losing dignity.

Wholeness creates balance. Each partner gives from overflow, not emptiness. They pour into each other, but neither one leaks. Their love doesn't demand; it invites. It doesn't confine; it cultivates.

> *"Whole partners don't complete each other; they cultivate each other."*

Commitment as Choice, Not Chain

Commitment in wholeness is a liberating covenant, not a confining cage. It doesn't restrict; it refines. The immature view of commitment says, *"I have to stay."* The mature view says, *"I choose to stay."*

In broken relationships, commitment often feels like captivity because it's built on fear: fear of loss, failure, or loneliness. In whole relationships, commitment feels like *freedom* because it's built on faith.

When love matures, it becomes a conscious choice renewed every day. It's not about enduring misery or suppressing individuality; it's about participating willingly in something sacred. Choice preserves intimacy, while obligation breeds resentment.

God never forces love. He invites it. Likewise, whole commitment mirrors divine love: a continual invitation to grow together in purpose and peace.

> *"Commitment isn't about possession; it's about participation."*

Aligning Your "Yes" with Divine Purpose

Every commitment carries spiritual weight. When you say *"yes"* to someone, you're also saying *"yes"* to the purpose that union will fulfill. That's why your *yes* must be aligned with divine order, not just emotional desire.

Before you commit, ask:

- Does this connection draw me closer to God or distract me from Him?
- Does it amplify my peace or constantly drain it?
- Does it challenge me to grow or tempt me to shrink?

When your *yes* aligns with divine purpose, love becomes a ministry, not just a feeling. It becomes a sacred partnership where both people are accountable to God for how they handle each other's hearts.

Whole commitment says *yes* not to fantasy, but to faith. It's the meeting point between spiritual maturity and relational readiness, the place where love transcends chemistry and becomes covenant.

> *"When your yes aligns with divine purpose, love becomes your ministry."*

Commitment Reimagined

Commitment in wholeness is a sacred exchange between two people who know they are already complete in God. Their union doesn't erase individuality; it elevates it. It doesn't replace identity; it refines it.

Whole love doesn't ask, *"Will this person complete me?"* It asks, *"Can we together complete what God has called us to do?"*

When our commitments are born of healing, sustained by honesty, and guided by divine order, love ceases to be fragile. It becomes fortified and whole instead. Once we discern the difference between interest, involvement and investment, we gain a clearer understanding of what real commitment and a whole relationship truly is.

When we heal from our brokenness and clarify our understanding of commitment, we free ourselves to love from truth rather than trauma. Yet even healthy commitment must follow divine sequence. Love thrives in order, the same order God used to form creation: purpose before partnership and foundation before fulfillment.

As we move forward, we'll explore what it means to do things in order — how divine design governs not just who we love, but *when* and *how* we align with them. When our commitments flow in God's timing, they bring peace instead of pressure, purpose instead of confusion, and covenant instead of chaos.

19

DOING THINGS IN ORDER

Order matters to God. From the galaxies to the human body, everything He created operates within divine design and sequence. Light came before life. Formation came before function. Purpose came before partnership. Likewise, in relationships, divine order brings peace, protection, and power.

When we step outside of that order, we may still experience connection but not covenant. We may experience pleasure, but not peace. Wholeness requires alignment with the way God designed love to unfold spiritually, emotionally, and physically in its proper time and sequence.

Divine Design of Relational Order

Divine order begins with wholeness in self and obedience to God. A relationship built in divine order follows the pattern of creation: first, God forms and then He fills. He forms our hearts, identity, and character, and only then fills our lives with companionship, covenant, and calling.

When we rush the process or rearrange the order, we invite disorder into what was meant to be sacred. In the world's system, attraction comes first, then attachment, then assessment. In God's design, *assessment* and *alignment* come first before *attachment* and *affection.* This is why understanding the phases of love matters.

Divine order doesn't suppress passion; it sanctifies it. God is not trying to withhold joy. He's trying to preserve it. When we surrender to His order, love becomes something deeper than desire. It becomes destiny.

Letting God Do the Choosing

When we allow God to choose our mates rather than relying on our short-sighted ideals, tastes, or affinities, we begin with God in the lead. Our emotions can be persuasive, but they are often temporary; God's perspective, however, is eternal. He knows the character, calling, and spiritual compatibility that we cannot yet see. When we surrender the selection process to Him, we invite divine foresight into our love story.

Operating in wholeness, as reflected in 1 Thessalonians 5:23, which prays that our "whole spirit, soul, and body be kept blameless," means living in harmony and completeness that mirrors God's original design. Wholeness positions us to discern clearly and to attract rightly. A whole person doesn't seek someone to complete them; they seek someone to complement the work God has already begun.

When God is in the picking, we don't just fulfill our personal desires; we fulfill His purpose. Our relationships become part of His larger promise to prosper us and give us peace (Jeremiah 29:11). His pairing produces unity, not confusion; purpose, not distraction; and peace, not turmoil.

We must never choose a mate on impulse and then ask God to bless what He never ordained. Too often, we make emotional decisions and then pray for divine endorsement, asking God to fix the very thing we built without His blueprint or blessing. If He didn't authorize or ordain something, it will lack His backing. His blessings flow through obedience, not resistance. When we let Him lead from the beginning, we avoid the pain of asking Him to repair what He never initiated.

When we choose by sight, we often chase chemistry. When we allow God to choose, we discover covenant.

Commitment and Consummation

Whether you understand this spiritually, practically, or otherwise, commitment should come before consummation. This is why the **phases of love** matter, so that you're not confused or prematurely entangled. Forming a physical connection activates powerful spiritual, psychological, and emotional bonds, so it must be preceded by fully committed individuals who understand and respect covenant. Without two whole, committed people, intimacy often leads to *fragmentation*, a false sense of union that eventually reveals underlying brokenness.

Physical intimacy is sacred, not evil. When sacred acts are performed outside of sacred context, they create bleak consequences rather than blessed covenant. True consummation should affirm what has already been committed, not compensate for what hasn't been clarified.

Holy Bonds vs. Unholy Bonds

We should be focusing on the *spirit* of the law ("no unholy bonds") rather than the *letter* ("no fornication"). The spirit of the law focuses on *intent and impact*, or why God set boundaries and how violating them affects the soul. The letter of the law focuses on *restriction* itself, which often produces circumstantial guilt without lasting transformation.

Paul stated, *"Do you not know that your bodies are members of Christ? Shall I then take the members of Christ and make them members of a harlot? Certainly not! Or do you not know that he who is joined to a harlot is one body with her? For 'the two,' He says, 'shall become one flesh.' But he who is joined to the Lord is one spirit with Him"* (1 Corinthians 6:15–17).

Paul's point is that the act of sexual intimacy creates a bond between two individuals. It's spiritual, as well as physical. The soul ties that form outside of divine order can entangle us emotionally, spiritually, and even mentally, making it harder to detach or discern. These unholy bonds often masquerade as love but produce anxiety, confusion, or dependency instead of peace, clarity, and growth.

A spiritual bond formed in divine order, however, aligns with God's covenant. It produces fruit, such as trust, stability, joy, and purpose. The difference is not just in the act but in the *authority* under which the act occurs. When God is present, love multiplies. When He's absent, love diminishes.

Unholy bonds keep us tied to what God is trying to free us from; holy bonds tie us to what God is trying to grow within us.

> *"Divine order protects what emotion alone cannot sustain."*

Doing Things in Order: The Wholeness Principle

Doing things in order is not about religious control; it's about spiritual protection. God's order shields us from unnecessary pain and emotional fragmentation. It preserves clarity, nurtures peace, and creates an atmosphere where love can flourish without fear.

When we skip steps, we often confuse chemistry with connection and intention with actual commitment. However, when we follow divine order, every stage of love builds on the previous one: trust before touch, prayer before passion, and purpose before pairing.

Doing things in order is how we honor God's blueprint for wholeness in love. It's how we ensure that what begins in passion can mature into purpose and that what begins in attraction can end in anointing.

20

THE X-FACTOR: GOD AT THE CENTER

When we begin with God's order and trust His selection, we make room for His presence to sustain what He has ordained. That's where divine partnership begins, and when whole love moves from order to oneness.

With God at the center of a whole relationship, love takes on divine order. Divine order doesn't mean hierarchy or control; it means alignment. It means each person seeks to love, serve, and support the other from a place of obedience to God's will rather than personal desire. In divine partnership, both individuals recognize that they are stewards, not owners, of one another's hearts. They understand that love is sacred trust, not emotional possession.

In human relationships, disorder often begins when one person becomes the "center." Whether it's ego, ambition or insecurity, misplaced focus leads to imbalance. However, when God is the focal point, both individuals orbit around a stable source of wisdom, power, and truth. The relationship becomes triangular with each person drawing closer to God individually, which in turn draws them closer to one another.

Having a healthy relationship without God in the center is possible, but it's not ideal. Having a Christ-centered relationship guarantees the possibility of gaining insight from the Creator of relationships Himself. Throughout Scripture, God reveals His design for love and partnership using His relationship with humanity as the ultimate example. Through His dealings with Israel and the Church, He teaches us about loyalty, sacrifice, devotion, mercy, forgiveness, and unwavering commitment.

God called the Israelites "adulterers," not because they broke a rule, but because they broke His heart. In Jeremiah 3:8–9 and Ezekiel 16, He accuses them of spiritual adultery for turning to other gods and abandoning their covenant with Him. The Prophet Hosea's marriage to Gomer, who was likened to the Israelites, serves as a living parable of that betrayal. Yet, like Hosea, even in our unfaithfulness, God's love remains. This is the essence of divine love: a love that endures betrayal, disappointment, and distance, and still chooses restoration over rejection.

Surviving but Not Thriving

A relationship can survive without God's presence, and it may even appear successful by worldly standards. People can cohabitate peacefully, share affection, raise families, and build businesses together. Without the sustaining grace of God, human love reaches its limit. It can't bear the weight of disappointment, betrayal, illness, or prolonged uncertainty.

God's love, however, is infinite, for it renews, heals, and restores. Without Him, couples often recycle the same conflicts or lean on temporary fixes: communication strategies, counseling or compromises that never address the root — disconnection from the Source. When God is absent, love becomes transactional. When God is present, love becomes transformational.

Thriving comes from alignment, not effort. A relationship thrives when the couple invites the Holy Spirit to dwell within it, guiding decisions, softening hearts, and revealing truth before bitterness takes root. The Spirit convicts gently, reminding both people of their divine identity and calling them to higher expressions of patience, forgiveness, and grace.

The Holy Spirit as the Third Strand in the Cord

Ecclesiastes 4:12 says, *"A cord of three strands is not easily broken."* The third strand in a whole relationship is the Holy Spirit, which is God's active presence binding two hearts in unity. Without that strand, love frays under pressure. With it, there is resilience, discernment, and supernatural peace.

The Holy Spirit interprets what words can't express, intercedes when communication breaks down, and brings clarity when emotions cloud judgment. He becomes the counselor, comforter, and glue that holds love together when human effort fails.

A couple led by the Spirit prays together, not as a ritual but as a lifeline. They don't seek perfection, but rather presence. They don't try to fix each other. Instead, they surrender together. In that surrender, love becomes something divine, rooted in purpose, not performance.

Faith, Wisdom, and the Counsel of the World

Some may wonder: If God should be at the center of our relationships, does that mean we ignore all human wisdom, such as behavioral theories, psychological research or practical advice? Scripture cautions us, *"Blessed is the man who walks not in the counsel of the ungodly"* (Psalm 1:1). However, that doesn't mean rejecting all natural insight; it means discerning its source and spirit.

The world's knowledge can observe what God has already designed, but it can't replace His wisdom. God's intelligence and creativity are evident in every part of creation, including biology, psychology, chemistry, and even the study of human emotion. Science is simply humanity's attempt to explain and uncover the magnificence of the Creator.

Therefore, relational theories such as **attachment styles**, **love languages** or **emotional intelligence** can be helpful, for they give us language to describe what we feel and frameworks to understand behavior. They can be the *first word* in awareness and analysis, but they should never be the *final word* in authority. God's Word and will must always remain the ultimate measure of truth.

When we keep God as the final authority, He helps us filter secular insight through divine wisdom. He reveals what aligns with His design and what distracts from it. As Proverbs 2:6 reminds us, *"For the Lord gives wisdom; from His mouth come knowledge and understanding."*

So, while research and theories can inform how we love, only revelation can transform *why* we love. The best of human understanding becomes most powerful when it bows to divine revelation.

When we integrate faith and wisdom this way, we not only practice love intelligently, but we also practice it spiritually. And prayer is the meeting place where the two worlds of science and spirit become one.

The Prayer of Whole Love

Prayer is not merely a ritual; it is the language of alignment. It invites God into the spaces where our strength ends and His wisdom begins. Through prayer, we welcome divine partnership, allowing the Holy Spirit to intervene, interpret, and inspire unity. When couples pray together, they do more than communicate with God; they commune with Him. Prayer becomes the sacred bridge between two hearts and Heaven.

It is through prayer that we invite God not only to bless the relationship but to govern it, sitting at the head rather than the sidelines. Prayer centers love in divine truth, humbles the ego, and restores clarity when emotions blur understanding. It's where we learn to listen for direction instead of demanding outcomes.

When two people pray together in sincerity, they realign with God's purpose and each other's peace. They begin to see conflict through the lens of grace, correction through compassion, and love through the eyes of eternity. Prayer makes space for the supernatural, transforming human affection into holy connection.

> *"A relationship centered on God becomes stronger than the two people within it."*

Prayer of Whole Love

Heavenly Father,

Thank You for being the author of love and the architect of divine partnership. We invite You to stand at the center of our relationship, governing our hearts, our home, and our choices. Teach us to love one another as You have loved us: faithfully, sacrificially, and without fear.
Where there is pride, plant humility. Where there is confusion, bring clarity. Where there is weariness, breathe new strength.

Let our connection reflect Your covenant and our affection reveal Your grace. Make us one in spirit, purpose, and peace.
May the Holy Spirit bind us together, anchoring us in faith, guarding us in truth, and guiding us in love.

We surrender our will to Yours, trusting that what You join together, no one can tear apart.

In Jesus' name, Amen.

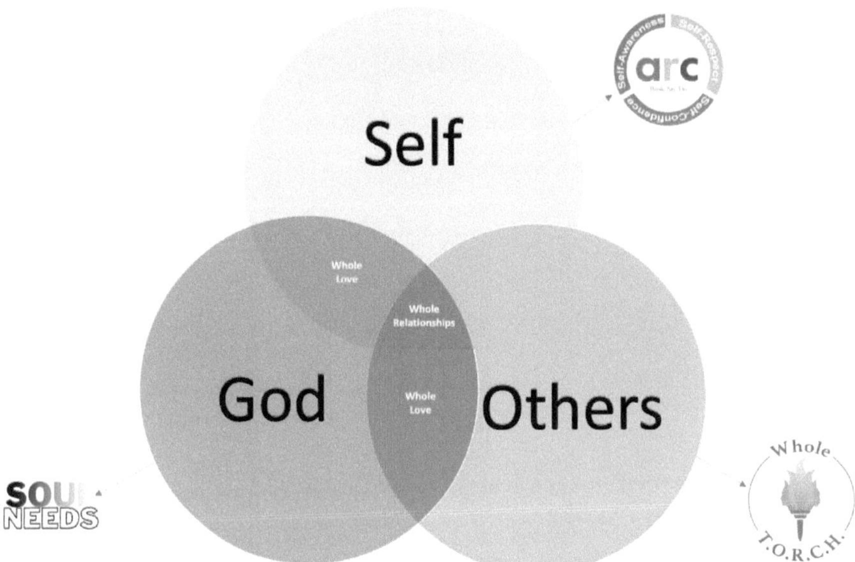
Self
Whole Love
Whole Relationships
God
Whole Love
Others
arc
Self-Awareness
Self-Respect
Self-Confidence
NEEDS
Whole
T.O.R.C.H.

21

LIVING WHOLE: LOVE THAT ENDURES

Living and loving whole means choosing reverence over pride, grace over ego, and understanding over accusation. Wholeness in love does not mean the absence of discomfort, however. It means the ability to handle it wisely. Every relationship will face challenge; conflict is as natural as breathing. The real test is not whether disagreements arise but how they are addressed.

Conflict, the Refining Fire of Love

Most of us don't truly want love; we want comfort. We crave the kind of ease that feels safe, predictable, and affirming. As long as things are smooth, we assume love is present. However, the moment conflict, challenge, or discomfort arises, we question the relationship or believe love has vanished.

The truth is that love isn't tested by the *absence* of conflict but by how two people navigate it together. The way you handle disagreement reveals the maturity of your connection. Does your partner attack, withdraw, or punish with silence? Or do they invite honesty and vulnerability, creating space to heal what's been hurt?

Many of us unconsciously seek partners who will soothe our insecurities or rescue us from discomfort, rather than those who will lovingly challenge our growth. Yet intimacy isn't born from the avoidance of pain; it's born from the courage to face it together. The deepest form of love doesn't deny brokenness; it redeems it.

Conflict, when handled with grace, becomes a refining fire. It purifies intentions, strengthens trust, and deepens connection. A loving partner acts as both mirror and mentor, reflecting the parts of us that need healing and teaching us how to love more honestly. True intimacy isn't destroyed by conflict; it is defined by the repair that follows it.

Danger vs. Discomfort

There's a critical difference between "**danger"** and "**discomfort"** and confusing the two can sabotage connection, growth, and healing.

Danger means there is a threat of real harm. Discomfort means emotional activation (i.e. shame, jealousy). When we are in danger, we need to seek safety or leave the situation. When we are discomforted or uncomfortable, we should reflect and communicate by listening and asking questions.

Discomfort is not the same as danger. Don't let discomfort trick you into believing you're unsafe and you must leave or escape. If you do, you might:

- Mistake safety for isolation
- Confuse peace with boredom or suspicion
- Avoid growth and call it self-protection
- Prematurely end relationships that could have deepened

Being emotionally *triggered* (i.e. feeling disrespected) doesn't automatically mean you're in danger. Feelings are data, not facts, and recognition of feelings doesn't mean reality. Just because something feels true doesn't mean it is. If you've lived in survival mode long enough, for instance, even peace can feel suspicious.

Danger	Discomfort
There's a real threat of harm	Emotional activation (e.g., shame, jealousy, fear)
Requires **exit, boundaries, or safety**	Calls for **curiosity, communication, reflection**
Survival mode is necessary	Growth mode is possible

When every emotional trigger gets treated like a red flag, you'll end up calling **avoidance "peace"** and **numbing "safety."** That's not healing; it's hiding.

Ask Yourself:

- Am I in real danger or just feeling something I'd rather not feel?
- Will leaving make me safe or just keep me comfortable?
- Is this about self-protection or self-sabotage?

If I still want to leave, then leave. This is not about forcing yourself to stay; it's about learning *why* you want to go. Furthermore, sometimes leaving ***is*** the right choice, but healing means you can tell the difference between: Avoiding Danger vs. Avoiding Discomfort

If you always leave when things get hard, you're not just avoiding **pain**, you're avoiding **progress**. Long-term relationships require navigating conflict, misunderstandings, and discomfort through "communication." That includes vulnerability, accountability, and a willingness to work through problems, not punish each other with silence or ultimatums. Healthy boundaries are one thing, but emotional shutdowns used to punish or control are another.

When your soul needs or personal boundaries are ignored, it breeds resentment. If left unspoken, resentment hardens into distance. It festers until it erupts, often in ways that seem sudden or out of proportion. Healthy, whole love speaks up with humility, not hostility, before emotions build into emotional debt. In summary:

- Discomfort is a signal, not a stop sign.
- Danger means protect yourself.
- Discomfort means pay attention.
- Healing is learning to stay present when it's safe, even if it's uncomfortable.

If you are re-evaluating past choices or relationships through this lens, pause here and write about what you now see more clearly and what you are choosing to release.

Avoidance vs. Accountability

Emotional *avoidance* refers to *the* deliberate *effort* to suppress, ignore or distract oneself *from* experiencing certain *emotions*. Avoidance, defensiveness, and denial may feel like protection, but they are actually barriers to intimacy.

In relationships, consistent avoidance of important emotional conversations can lead to feelings of invalidation, resentment, and disconnection for the person whose feelings are being avoided. The impact is often that the other person feels their feelings are not important or are being dismissed. For someone who carries rejection or abandonment wounds, being dismissed, even unintentionally, can reawaken deep insecurities. That's why ghosting, avoidance, stonewalling, or blocking are toxic responses to discomfort; they silence the heart that most needs to feel seen.

Avoidance can be driven by various factors, and its effect on others' feelings can vary depending on the context and intent. A person might avoid a difficult conversation without consciously trying to invalidate the other person's feelings. Their focus may be entirely on managing their own distress, even if the end result unfortunately makes the other person feel dismissed. Here are some common reasons for avoidance:

- **Coping mechanism:** Avoidance can be a way of coping with anxiety, fear, or stress when faced with difficult emotions or confrontation. The person may simply feel overwhelmed and lack the tools to manage the situation effectively in that moment.
- **Emotional regulation strategy:** For some, avoidance serves, often unconsciously, as a way to regulate intense emotions. When something feels too painful or threatening to face, withdrawing becomes a temporary form of self-protection, even if it ultimately causes harm.
- **Punishment or control:** In other cases, avoidance is used intentionally to manipulate emotional outcomes. The "silent treatment" or emotional withdrawal may be employed to punish, control, or coerce desired behavior. This form of emotional blackmail uses affection and attention as currency, reinforcing dependency rather than connection.

Whether driven by fear or control, the goal of avoidance is usually the same: to protect oneself from emotional overload by escaping. Yet avoidance doesn't protect the relationship; it postpones its healing.

Accountability is the antidote. It requires courage to acknowledge your actions, take ownership of your mistakes and "lean into the discomfort" rather than retreat from it. Accountability restores trust where avoidance erodes it. It says, *"I care enough to face this with you, even when it's hard."*

Accountability involves two crucial elements:

- "I'm sorry" – Acknowledging that harm was done, taking responsibility, and expressing remorse.
- "I understand" – Demonstrating empathy and awareness of the impact of your actions, not just that you caused harm, but how and why it hurt the other person or affected the situation.

Thus, accountability is **"I'm sorry"** ***plus*** **"I understand."** Without both, accountability often falls short. For example:

- If you only say "I'm sorry" but don't show understanding, it can feel hollow or performative.
- If you only say "I understand" without remorse, it can come across as cold or dismissive.

Together, they reflect real ownership and the potential for change. To live whole is to respond consciously, not reactively, recognizing that both truth and tenderness are required for healing communication.

Whole love doesn't hide from discomfort; it grows through it. When both partners choose accountability over avoidance, they create a space where honesty becomes healing and connection becomes enduring. Over time, accountability does more than repair relationships; it reshapes how pain is held and how meaning is formed.

Healing rarely moves in a straight line, and wholeness does not arrive all at once. Once healing has eventually been integrated into wholeness ("whole healing"), it often reveals itself through a few recurring movements: the ability to find levity where pain once ruled, the willingness to extract wisdom from what was endured, the courage to choose love over bitterness, the resolve to live differently because of what was learned, and, for some, the calling to turn personal experience into service for others. These movements do not erase the past or minimize harm. They redeem it by allowing pain to be integrated rather than avoided. When healing reaches this point, identity is no longer shaped by what happened, but by how truth, love, and purpose have been allowed to emerge from it.

> *"Whole love is not something you feel; it is something you live."*

The workbook contains invaluable exercise on the Five L's of Whole Healing. Laughter, learning, love, living anew, and launching purpose are not steps to rush through, but signs that healing has begun to integrate into identity.

Gratitude as the Elixir

When healing has been integrated and meaning has emerged, gratitude becomes the posture that keeps wholeness from hardening into pride or grief into bitterness. Gratitude is the great elixir of love. It soothes the mind, quiets the ego, and heals the fractures caused by misunderstanding. When you practice appreciation for the blessings and lessons of your relationship – no matter how small – you shift from defensiveness to openness, from entitlement to humility. Gratitude softens the heart and reminds you that love itself is a gift, not a guarantee.

Gratitude prevents one of the most common dangers in any relationship: taking others for granted. It invites us to notice what is often overlooked or treated as common. This could be someone's steady consideration, everyday gestures, or just the simple presence of another soul walking beside us. In this way, we remember how sacred people and their presence truly are.

A grateful heart cannot hold bitterness for long. It keeps your tone gentle and your perspective grounded in grace. Gratitude doesn't deny what hurts; it reframes it. It says, *"Even here, there is something to learn. Even this can serve my growth."*

Gratitude keeps your heart hopeful, your tone gentle, and your love resilient. It is both a healing balm and a preventative medicine against bitterness. It transforms ordinary moments into sacred ones and reminds both partners that every day together is another chance to honor the divine within each other.

Gratitude, then, is not just a feeling. It's a spiritual practice that keeps love whole.

When Self-Work Becomes Soul Service

Wholeness begins with self-work but matures into soul service. It starts when two imperfect people commit not to *complete* each other but to *contribute* to each other's growth. In a whole relationship, love is not a transaction of needs but a transformation of souls.

When you are self-aware, you recognize your triggers, patterns, and limitations. You know where your wounds are and no longer ask your partner to heal what only you and God can. You become responsible for your energy and intentional with your actions. Self-awareness is how you bring truth into the relationship. It is the mirror you hold up for yourself before trying to reflect your partner.

When you are surrendered, you let love flow through you rather than trying to control its direction. Surrender isn't weakness; it's wisdom. It means you trust the process more than your pride and choose humility over being "right." Surrender creates space for God to work in and through the relationship.

When you are willing to serve, you view your partner's soul as sacred territory. You learn to ask, *"What does their soul need right now?"* instead of *"What do I want from them?"* Sometimes that need is compassion. Sometimes it's truth. Sometimes it's space to heal. Servanthood means showing up for each other with reverence, not rescue, expressing a whole love that uplifts rather than controls.

Two imperfect people, when self-aware, surrendered, and willing to serve, form the living embodiment of a whole relationship. They become mirrors of grace, reminding each other who they are and whose they are. Together they build not a perfect union, but a holy one where love is both the lesson and the legacy.

Living and Loving Whole

Whole love is something we become, not something we find. It begins within where healing softens what was hardened, and grace fills what was empty. As we learn to love ourselves in truth, we become capable of loving others in freedom.

Wholeness is not perfection; it is integration. It is the sacred meeting place where our humanity and divinity embrace, where two imperfect souls, aware of their flaws yet surrendered to their purpose, learn to serve one another's becoming.

When self-work turns into soul service, love becomes holy ground. It is no longer about possession or performance but partnership and purpose. It is a reflection of divine reciprocity, the love that flows through us, not just to us.

To live whole is to love as God loves: patiently, truthfully, and without fear. It is to see every relationship as both mirror and ministry, every wound as an invitation to grow, and every act of forgiveness as an altar of renewal.

In the end, wholeness is a journey expressed in how we connect and commit to ourselves and others. It is a lifelong practice of returning to whole love again and again until love itself becomes who we are.

Wholeness is not a destination you reach; it is a way of living to which you return routinely. Thus, the workbook's practices are meant to be revisited as often as needed. Let them become part of your rhythm rather than a task you complete.

A whole relationship does not mean two people who never struggle. It means two people who are honest enough to tell the truth, humble enough to repair what breaks, and secure enough to let each other grow.

In a whole relationship, both people know who they are. They communicate clearly, respect boundaries, and take responsibility for their emotions. Conflict does not destroy the relationship because trust is stronger than fear. Two whole people do not try to complete one another. They bring their wholeness to the relationship and build something stronger together – an unbroken love.

PART V REVIEW: THE PRACTICE OF WHOLENESS

Wholeness is a daily practice. It is a lifestyle we commit to living with awareness, surrender, and service. Part V guided you through the practical rhythms of this whole love lifestyle:

- moving from attraction to authentic commitment,
- healing from premature or misplaced attachments,
- following divine order instead of emotional impulse,
- letting God choose what your heart cannot discern alone,
- and building a relationship where the Holy Spirit remains the third strand.

You also learned how to distinguish danger from discomfort, how to remain present through conflict rather than avoiding it, and how gratitude becomes the quiet strength that sustains enduring love.

By this point in the journey, the full picture of wholeness becomes clear. You began by understanding brokenness and reclaiming your identity through the ARC of Self. You then explored the soul needs that shape our desires and behaviors. From there, you learned how wholeness expresses itself through the TORCH of Love in relationship with others. Finally, Part V revealed what it means to live that love faithfully through commitment.

Whole love is not simply something you feel. It is something you practice, protect, and live.

This final section prepares you not only to understand wholeness, but to embody it in the relationships you build and the life you continue to shape.

Now that you grasp what living whole means, review the affirmations in ***Appendix E*** *that support maintaining a whole relationship. For journal prompts to continue your journey into a committed whole love, visit* ***Appendix F****.*

ACKNOWLEDGMENT OF THE WHOLE JOURNEY

You have walked through the landscapes of love, loss, reflection, and renewal. Along the way, you've been invited to see yourself more clearly, to heal more honestly, and to love more wholly. Remember, wholeness is not a destination but a daily devotion, an ever-deepening practice of awareness, surrender, and service.

May the truths in these pages continue to meet you in new ways as you grow. May you carry this work into your relationships, your communities, and the quiet corners of your soul. May you come to know that the journey toward wholeness was never about perfection, but rather presence: the courage to keep choosing love.

Always remember, you do not find wholeness in love. You bring wholeness to love.

Whole Benediction

We do not arrive at wholeness;
we awaken to it
each time we choose
love over control,
grace over pride,
and faith over doubt.

Whole Affirmation

Say the following affirmation out loud, write it down, or pair it with breathwork as a daily routine, believing every word to be true.

"I am whole; therefore, I can love wholly."

Get more information and resources on the website: **www.wholerelationship.com**

AUTHOR'S NOTE

Thank you for taking this journey with me. Writing *Whole Relationships* has been as much an act of healing as it has been of teaching. Each page has reminded me that love is a living practice, one that begins within but never ends there.

My hope is that this book meets you where you are and gently points you toward who you are becoming. Whether you are mending a relationship, deepening one, or simply learning to be whole on your own, may these insights serve as companions on your path.

If you wish to continue this work, the *Whole Relationships* workbook offers guided reflections, practical exercises, and soul-alignment tools to help you apply these principles in daily life. I invite you to use it, share it, and live it because every act of love, awareness, surrender, and service brings more wholeness into the world.

With gratitude and grace,
Annette R. Purkiss

APPENDICES

Appendix A: Brokenness Diagnostic Quiz

Purpose:
This brief quiz is designed to help you quickly recognize whether your current relationship patterns are being shaped by unhealed wounds, emotional clarity, or genuine wholeness. There are no right or wrong answers, only honest ones. Awareness is the first step toward alignment.

Instructions:
Answer each question **Yes** or **No**.
Be honest. Respond based on your *current* relational patterns, not who you hope to be.

THE QUIZ

1. **Do you ignore your own needs to keep the peace or avoid conflict?**
   Yes / No

2. **Do you feel anxious, insecure or uncertain when someone doesn't respond quickly or the way you hoped?**
   Yes / No

3. **Do you stay in relationships where you are not valued, respected or emotionally supported?**
   Yes / No

4. **Do you struggle to set boundaries or feel guilty when you do?**
   Yes / No

5. **Do you find yourself repeating the same relational patterns, even when you know they're unhealthy?**
   Yes / No

6. **Do you overgive, overfunction, or overcompensate to prove your worth in relationships?**
   Yes / No

7. **Do you shut down, withdraw or avoid vulnerability because it feels unsafe?**
   Yes / No

8. **Do you feel triggered by small things that feel bigger than the moment?**
   Yes / No

9. **Do you choose partners or friendships that reflect your wounds more than your worth?**
   Yes / No

10. **Do you struggle to trust yourself to make good decisions in love?**
   Yes / No

SCORING

Count the number of **Yes** answers.

0–3 YES answers: Operating From WHOLENESS

You are grounded, discerning, and emotionally aware.

Your choices reflect clarity, values, and healthy self-worth.

Continue nurturing this alignment. It is the foundation of unbroken love.

4–6 YES answers: Operating From HEALING

You are aware of your patterns, and that awareness is creating meaningful change.

You're not where you once were, and not yet where you're going, but you are evolving.

This is a sacred transition. Lean into intentional growth as you move toward wholeness.

7–10 YES answers: Operating From BROKENNESS

Your relational patterns may be shaped by past hurts, unmet needs, or unhealed wounds.

This does not make you flawed; it makes you human.

Brokenness simply means something in your inner world needs attention, compassion, and alignment.

You are not stuck. You are becoming aware, and awareness is the beginning of freedom.

NEXT STEPS

If you scored in the Healing or Brokenness range, your next step is clear: Turn to **Appendix B: The Whole Relationship Self-Assessment** for a deeper exploration of the five dimensions of wholeness.

You may also find it helpful to revisit:

- Chapter 2: Brokenness — How We Lose Ourselves in Love
- Appendix C: ARC & TORCH Language Charts
- Appendix D: Soul Needs Discovery Worksheet

Your wholeness journey begins with one brave "Yes," the one you just gave yourself.

APPENDIX B: THE WHOLE RELATIONSHIP SELF-ASSESSMENT

Purpose:
This assessment helps you evaluate the condition of your inner world and the patterns you bring into relationships. Wholeness is alignment, not perfection. The more aligned your thoughts, emotions, behaviors, values, and identity become, the more capable you are of creating unbroken love with another person.

Instructions:
For each statement, rate yourself from 1 to 5:

1 = Strongly Disagree

2 = Disagree

3 = Neutral or Sometimes

4 = Agree

5 = Strongly Agree

SECTION 1 — BODY (Behavioral Wholeness)

Your habits, boundaries, consistency, and actions

1. I keep the promises I make to myself.
2. My daily habits support my emotional and spiritual well-being.
3. I set and maintain healthy boundaries without guilt.
4. I recognize when my behavior is harming me or others and make adjustments.
5. I follow through on commitments even when my emotions fluctuate.

SECTION 2 — MIND (Cognitive Wholeness)

Your thoughts, beliefs, clarity, and self-perception

6. I can clearly identify the beliefs that shape how I love and relate to others.
7. I challenge unhelpful thoughts instead of accepting them automatically.
8. I make decisions from clarity, not fear or insecurity.
9. I understand the patterns that tend to repeat in my relationships.
10. I can articulate what I need without overthinking or confusion.

SECTION 3 — HEART (Emotional Wholeness)

Your empathy, honesty, connection, and vulnerability

11. I am honest with myself about my emotions.
12. I express my feelings in healthy, respectful ways.
13. I allow myself to be vulnerable with people who earn my trust.
14. I recognize when my emotional reactions are connected to past wounds.
15. I seek connection, not control or validation.

SECTION 4 — SPIRIT (Value-Centered Wholeness)

Your alignment with purpose, conviction, principles, and faith

16. My relationships reflect my values, not my wounds.
17. I seek divine wisdom or intuition before making major decisions.
18. I choose partners who honor my worth and respect my principles.
19. I can distinguish between what feels good and what is truly good for me.
20. I pursue relationships that elevate my growth and character.

SECTION 5 — SOUL (Identity Wholeness)

Your sense of self, worth, belonging, and authentic identity

21. I know who I am outside of my relationships.
22. I do not lose myself trying to keep someone else.
23. I can recognize when my soul needs rest, support, or recalibration.
24. I feel grounded in my purpose and the "why" behind my life.
25. I show up in relationships as my whole, authentic self.

SCORING

Add your scores for each section:

BODY Score: _____ / 25

MIND Score: _____ / 25

HEART Score: _____ / 25

SPIRIT Score: _____ / 25

SOUL Score: _____ / 25

TOTAL Score: _____ / 125

INTERPRETATION: The Wholeness Spectrum

100–125: WHOLE

You live with clarity, emotional maturity, healthy boundaries, and a grounded inner life. You are capable of building whole, reciprocal, God-centered relationships.

75–99: FLOURISHING

Your foundation is strong, and you are actively growing. A few areas may still need intentional strengthening, but you are moving steadily toward wholeness.

50–74: FORMING

You are in an important season of self-work and awareness. This is not weakness; it is opportunity. Healing and alignment in this stage lead to powerful transformation.

0–49: FRAGMENTED

Your inner world may feel disconnected, overwhelmed, or burdened. Begin gently. Awareness itself is a victory. Focus on one dimension at a time and revisit the tools in this book to rebuild stability and alignment.

NEXT STEPS

To deepen your growth:

- Revisit the ARC and TORCH frameworks throughout this book.
- Use the Soul Needs Discovery Worksheet (Appendix D).
- Apply the Daily Affirmations for Wholeness (Appendix E).
- Reflect using the Journal Prompts for Self & Relationship (Appendix F).

Your path to wholeness is continuous, intentional, and sacred.

APPENDIX C: ARC & TORCH LANGUAGE CHARTS

A quick-reference guide to everyday language that reflects alignment within yourself and connection with others.

THE ARC OF SELF

(Part II Framework)
Self-Awareness | Self-Respect | Self-Confidence

SELF-AWARENESS

- "I'm noticing…"
- "I've realized…"
- "I'm becoming aware that…"
- "I'm working on…"
- "I forgive myself for…"

SELF-RESPECT

- "I need…"
- "This doesn't work for me."
- "I'm choosing what's healthy for me."
- "That crosses a boundary for me."
- "I'm honoring my needs."

SELF-CONFIDENCE

- "I believe I can handle this."
- "I trust my judgment."
- "I'm capable of growing through this."
- "I can try again."
- "I'm stronger than this moment."

THE TORCH OF LOVE

(Part IV Framework)
Trust | Openness | Respect | Communication | Humility

TRUST

- "You can rely on me."
- "I give you my word."
- "I won't let you down."
- "You're safe with me."

OPENNESS

- "I need…"
- "I think…"
- "I feel…"
- "I want / I don't want…"

RESPECT

- "What do you need from me?"
- "I did this because it matters to you."
- "I chose not to do that because I know you wouldn't want it."
- "Your preferences are important to me."

COMMUNICATION

- "Let's talk."
- "I'm listening."
- "Let me explain…"
- "There's something you should know…"

HUMILITY

- "I'm sorry."
- "This part was my fault."
- "What do you think?"
- "I don't know, but I want to understand."

APPENDIX D: SOUL NEEDS DISCOVERY WORKSHEET

This is a guided reflection to help you understand the needs of your soul, such as what grounds you, what grows you, and what makes you uniquely whole.

Remember, your soul has **Universal Needs** (shared by all people) and **Unique Needs** (specific to who you are). This worksheet helps you identify both so you can build relationships that nourish your identity, honor your purpose, and support your growth.

SECTION 1 — UNIVERSAL SOUL NEEDS

Truth • Love • Faith

These needs belong to everyone. They are the foundation of a whole and grounded inner life.

Reflection Questions — TRUTH

1. Where do I need more truth in my life right now?
2. What truths about myself have I avoided or minimized?
3. How do I know when something aligns with my soul's truth?

Reflection Questions — LOVE

4. What forms of love strengthen me the most?
5. What forms of love drain me or make me smaller?
6. Do I give myself the love I easily give others? If not, why?

Reflection Questions — FAITH

7. What helps me feel spiritually grounded or connected?
8. What beliefs, promises, or scriptures keep me anchored?
9. Where is my faith asking me to grow, surrender, or trust?

SECTION 2 — UNIQUE SOUL NEEDS

Talent • Traits • Time

These needs arise from who you are: your unique design, temperament, gifts, and sacred wiring.

Reflection Questions — TALENT

10. What activities or abilities feel natural and energizing for me?
11. Which talents of mine have been underused or ignored lately?
12. How does my soul respond when I'm not able to use my gifts?

Reflection Questions — TRAITS

13. Which personality traits define me most strongly (e.g., gentle, bold, analytical, imaginative)?
14. Which traits feel misunderstood or undervalued by others?
15. What traits need more acceptance, development, or expression?

Reflection Questions — TIME

16. When do I feel most myself: morning, evening, late night, or during solitude?
17. How much unstructured time does my soul need to feel balanced?
18. Where is my time currently going that is draining me?

SECTION 3 — THE SOUL'S CENTER

Purpose • Personality • Perspective

This is the intersection where your Universal and Unique needs meet. It is the **core of who you are**, the place from which your relationships, decisions, and wholeness flow.

Guided Prompts

19. **Purpose:**
    What do I feel called to do, contribute, or become at this stage of my life?

20. **Personality:**
    Which parts of my personality feel most authentic and alive?
    Which parts have I hidden or suppressed?

21. **Perspective:**
    What worldview or lived experiences shape how I see myself and others?
    How is my perspective evolving as I heal and grow?

SECTION 4 — IDENTIFYING YOUR TOP 5 SOUL NEEDS

Based on your answers, list the five needs your soul is craving **right now** (not in the past, not ideally but right now).

1.
2.
3.
4.
5.

SECTION 5 — ALIGNMENT CHECK

Complete these final statements to bring your needs into clarity:

1. **My soul feels starved when...**

2. **My soul feels nourished when...**

3. **In this season, my soul most needs...**

4. **To honor my soul, I must stop...**

5. **To honor my soul, I must start...**

SECTION 6 — A FINAL SOUL AFFIRMATION

You may choose one or write your own.

- "My soul deserves what makes me whole."
- "I honor what I need without apology."
- "My soul is worthy of truth, love, faith, and time."
- "I am aligned with who I am becoming."
- "My soul's needs are sacred, and I listen."

Space to write your own:

APPENDIX E: DAILY AFFIRMATIONS FOR WHOLENESS

Words shape your inner world. Every time you speak life into yourself, you realign your mind, heart, spirit, and soul. Use these affirmations daily – morning, evening, or whenever you feel disconnected from your worth.

The affirmations are organized into the five Dimensions of Wholeness:

- **BODY (Behavior)**
- **MIND (Thoughts)**
- **HEART (Emotions)**
- **SPIRIT (Values & Faith)**
- **SOUL (Identity)**

You may speak one per day or choose the ones that meet your current season.

BODY — Behavioral Wholeness

Affirmations for boundaries, consistency, and healthy action.

- "I honor myself with my choices."
- "I keep the promises I make to myself."
- "My boundaries protect what is sacred within me."
- "I move with intention, not impulse."
- "I release habits that drain me and choose actions that nourish me."
- "I walk away from what harms my peace."
- "I do not abandon myself to be accepted by anyone."

MIND — Cognitive Wholeness

Affirmations for clarity, truth, and healthy thinking.

- "I think clearly. I choose wisely."
- "My thoughts work for me, not against me."

- "I see patterns, and I choose differently this time."
- "I am not defined by old stories; I create new meaning."
- "I trust my perception, even when others don't understand it."
- "Confusion is not God's language; clarity is."
- "I release the lies that kept me small."

HEART — Emotional Wholeness

Affirmations for vulnerability, self-compassion, and emotional honesty.

- "I am safe. I am whole. I am already enough."
- "I do not chase love; I remember that I am love."
- "My vulnerability is not my weakness; it is my witness."
- "My emotions speak wisdom, not shame."
- "I feel deeply, and that is a strength."
- "I honor what my heart knows."
- "The child within me deserves tenderness and protection."

SPIRIT — Value-Centered Wholeness

Affirmations for purpose, alignment, humility, and spiritual grounding.

- "I honor my divine design."
- "I no longer chase closure where God has granted clarity."
- "God guides my steps, even when I can't see the path ahead."
- "My worth is sacred; I do not negotiate it."
- "I choose what aligns with who God is shaping me to be."
- "I surrender what is not mine to carry."
- "I am growing into the person I was created to become."

SOUL — Identity Wholeness

Affirmations for purpose, self-worth, and sacred identity.

- "I am whole, even as I heal."
- "I am worthy of truth, love, faith, and rest."
- "I do not chase safety in others. I am safe within myself."
- "My soul is not desperate; it is discerning."

- "I belong to myself first."
- "My purpose is unfolding exactly as it should."
- "I show up as the fullest expression of who I am."
- I was created and formed by God with perfect intention, and I'm here because I have value to Him.

SIGNATURE AFFIRMATIONS

1. Choose the affirmation that speaks to your day.
2. Speak it slowly.
3. Believe it fully.
4. Repeat it routinely.
5. Let it anchor you in wholeness.

The Mirror of Awareness

- "I am safe. I am whole. I am already enough."
- "I do not chase love; I remember that I am love."

The Power of Self-Respect

- "I honor my divine design."
- "I no longer chase closure where God has granted clarity."
- "My worth is sacred, and I will not trade it for attention."

Confidence to Be Seen

- "My vulnerability is not my weakness; it's my witness."
- "I reveal my truth, and the right souls will meet me there."

Cultivating Internal Safety

- "I do not chase safety in others. I am safe and resist fear."

APPENDIX F: JOURNAL PROMPTS FOR SELF & RELATIONSHIP

Writing unlocks understanding, causing us to reflect and literally see our thoughts. These writing prompts help you explore the patterns, beliefs, emotions, and desires that shape how you love, choose, connect, and respond. Use them at your own pace. Let each question reveal truth, release tension, and realign you with wholeness.

1. EMOTIONAL HEALING

- What wounds do I keep reliving through my relationships?
- What emotions do I suppress to keep the peace?
- What does my body do when it feels unsafe even if my mind says "everything is fine"?
- Where am I still seeking closure that was already resolved in truth?
- What would emotional peace look like in this season of my life?

2. RELATIONSHIP DISCERNMENT

- What is this situation revealing about me?
- What lesson keeps repeating because I haven't learned it yet?
- What would I do differently if I already felt loved, secure, and whole?
- What patterns am I repeating from childhood or past relationships?
- What might God or life be trying to teach me through this emotional pattern?

3. INTERNAL SAFETY

- What does "safety" in a relationship actually look like for me?
- When I feel fear, what story am I telling myself?
- What would it look like to fully trust my intuition?
- Am I more familiar with emotional chaos than calm?
- How can I build a life that feels safe inside me first?

4. SELF-AWARENESS

- What part of me gets activated when someone pulls away?
- How old does that version of me feel? What does she fear?
- What truths about myself have I been avoiding?
- What belief is silently guiding my choices right now?
- What am I really seeking when I seek attention or validation?
- If my younger self could speak freely, what would she say?
- When have I outsourced my wholeness to outcomes or other people?

5. SELF-RESPECT

- In what ways have I accepted disrespect disguised as love or friendship?
- What part of me still believes I must earn love?
- When have I stayed somewhere that dishonored me and what fear kept me there?
- What does self-respect look like in my everyday choices?
- How can I remind myself that my worth is inherent, not conditional?
- Where do I still abandon myself to keep someone else comfortable?

6. SELF-CONFIDENCE

- What fears arise when I imagine being emotionally open with someone?
- How has withholding vulnerability protected me and what has it cost me?
- When was the last time vulnerability brought me clarity instead of pain?
- What does "being seen" mean to me?
- What risks would I take if I trusted myself more fully?

7. SOUL IDENTITY

- Who am I when no one needs anything from me?
- What parts of my identity have I hidden to be accepted?
- What does my soul crave that I've been ignoring?
- Which of my gifts have gone unused and how does that affect me?
- What perspective shift am I being invited into right now?

8. PATTERNS, TRIGGERS & GROWTH

- What situations consistently trigger me and why?
- Where do my emotional reactions feel larger than the moment?
- How do I typically soothe myself when I feel unsafe or unseen?
- What new pattern would serve me better?
- What would "growth" look like in action this week?

9. LOVE & CONNECTION

- How do I know when love is present and when it is absent?
- How do I show love, and how do I prefer to receive it?
- What does emotional reciprocity look like to me?
- What do I need from a relationship that I'm afraid to admit?
- What kind of love aligns with who I am becoming?

10. COMMITMENT & WHOLE LOVE

These are the questions people are afraid to ask but must answer before they enter whole love.

Readiness for Whole Love

- Am I ready to give love that is consistent, intentional, and reciprocal?
- What does long-term emotional maturity look like in my life right now?
- What habits or patterns would make commitment difficult for me today?
- If whole love requires honesty, where am I still hiding?
- Am I prepared to grow, stretch, apologize, and repair, not just feel?

Surrender & Letting Go of Ego

- What fears am I still holding that might sabotage intimacy?
- Where do I struggle to surrender control and why?
- What expectations or fantasies do I need to release to love someone real?
- Am I willing to let love teach me, even when the lesson is uncomfortable?
- Which parts of my heart resist vulnerability, closeness or dependence?

Mutual Servanthood

(Servanthood meaning: "I serve you without losing me. You serve me without losing you.")

- What does it mean for me to love someone in a way that elevates their soul?
- Where have I loved with performance instead of partnership?
- How can I practice servanthood without slipping into self-abandonment?
- What does it look like for someone to lovingly serve *me* in return?
- Am I ready to honor someone else's needs without resentment or fear?

Commitment as a Spiritual Choice

- What spiritual qualities do I want to bring into my next relationship?
- What kind of partner do I need to become to sustain whole love?
- What does God invite me to surrender, trust, or embrace in love?
- How do I define commitment, not from culture or fear, but from wholeness?
- Am I ready to choose someone, not because I need them, but because I align with them?
- In what ways can I invite God to be more central in my relationship, not just in crisis, but in daily connection?

FINAL REFLECTION

Choose one and journal your answer:

- "If I trusted myself completely, I would…"
- "If I honored my truth, I would…"
- "If I no longer operated from brokenness, I would…"
- "If I let God guide me, I would…"
- "If I loved myself fully, I would…"

Final Question (The Mirror of Commitment)

If whole love walked into my life tomorrow, would I be ready or would my fears, habits or wounds push it away somehow?

Ultimate Healing Challenge

If perfect, unconditional love could speak to the most broken area of my life to heal or restore me to wholeness, what would it say?

Write freely in your journal. Let truth answer, not fear.

BIBLIOGRAPHY

Bonner, Dale. Sermon delivered at Word of Faith Church, Austell, GA, November 5, 2025.

Brown, Brené. *Daring Greatly: How the Courage to Be Vulnerable Transforms the Way We Live, Love, Parent, and Lead*. New York: Gotham Books, 2012.

Burgoon, Judee K., and Aaron E. Bacue. "Nonverbal Communication Skills." In *Handbook of Communication and Social Interaction Skills*, edited by John O. Greene and Brant R. Burleson, 179–219. Mahwah, NJ: Lawrence Erlbaum Associates, 2003.

Chapman, Gary. *The 5 Love Languages: The Secret to Love that Lasts*. Chicago: Northfield Publishing, 2015.

Chapman, Gary, and Jennifer Thomas. *The Five Languages of Apology: How to Experience Healing in All Your Relationships*. Chicago: Northfield Publishing, 2006.

Chu, Charles and Lowrey, Brian S. "Self-Essentialist Reasoning Underlies the Similarity-Attraction Effect." *Journal of Personality and Social Psychology: Interpersonal Relations and Group Processes*, 125, no. 4 (2023): 601–618. https://www.apa.org/pubs/journals/releases/psp-pspi0000425.pdf

Frei, Jennifer R., and Phillip R. Shaver. "Respect in Close Relationships: Prototype Definition, Self-Report Assessment, and Initial Correlates." *Personal Relationships* 9, no. 2 (2002): 121–139. https://adultattachment.faculty.ucdavis.edu/wp-content/uploads/sites/66/2015/09/Frei_2002_Respect-in-close-relationships.pdf

Gottman, John M., & Silver, Nan. *The Seven Principles for Making Marriage Work: A Practical Guide from the Country's Foremost Relationship Expert*. New York: Harmony Books, 2015.

Gottman, J. M. *What Predicts Divorce?* Hillsdale, NJ: Erlbaum, 1994.

Gottman, J. M., Gottman, J. S., Cole, D. L., & Cole, C. U. *Handbook of Psychotherapy Case Formulation* (3rd ed.), 2022.

Gottman, J. M. & DeClaire, Joan. *The Relationship Cure:* A 5 Step Guide to Strengthening Your Marriage, Family, and Friendships. Harmony/Rodale/Convergent, 2001

Jensen, Nate. "Emotional Avoidance and Mental Well-Being." University of Oklahoma. Sept. 6, 2024 https://students.ouhsc.edu/news/articles/emotional-avoidance-and-mental-well-being

Johnson, Annette Purkiss. *What's Your Motivation?* Identifying and Understanding What Drives You (3rd Ed). Atlanta: Allwrite Publishing, 2026.

Johnson, Annette Purkiss. *The Five Ways We Work:* Unlock the Power of Knowing How You're Meant to Work. Atlanta: Allwrite Publishing, 2026.

Johnson, Sue. 2008. Hold Me Tight: Seven Conversations for a Lifetime of Love. New York: Little, Brown Spark.

Mehrabian, Albert. *Silent Messages.* Belmont, CA: Wadsworth, 1971.

Perel, Esther. "Appreciating Otherness in Relationships." Letters from Esther (blog), EstherPerel.com, August 30, 2023. https://www.estherperel.com/blog/letters-from-esther-30-appreciating-otherness-in-relationships

Perel, Esther. *Mating in Captivity: Unlocking Erotic Intelligence.* New York: HarperCollins, 2006.

Rosenberg, Marshall B. *Nonviolent Communication: A Language of Life.* Encinitas, CA: PuddleDancer Press, 2003.

Travers, Mark. "3 Subtle Signs That Your Partner Respects You, According to a Psychologist." Forbes, September 12, 2024. https://www.forbes.com/sites/traversmark/2025/09/12/3-subtle-signs-that-your-partner-respects-you-by-a-psychologist

www.ingramcontent.com/pod-product-compliance
Ingram Content Group UK Ltd.
Pitfield, Milton Keynes, MK11 3LW, UK
UKHW041856190726
13854UKWH00002B/936